The **Essential** B
FOR
MODEL T
All models 1909 to 1927

Your marque experts:
Chris Barker and Neil Tuckett

Essential Buyer's Guide Series

Alfa Romeo Alfasud – All saloon models from 1971 to 1983 & Sprint models from 1976 to 1989 (Metcalfe)
Alfa Romeo Giulia GT Coupé (Booker)
Alfa Romeo Giulia Spider (Booker & Talbott)
Audi TT – All Mk1 (8N) models: 1998-2006 (Davies)
Austin-Healey Big Healeys (Trummel)
BMW Boxer Twins – All air-cooled R45, R50, R60, R65, R75, R80, R90, R100, RS, RT & LS (Not GS) models 1969 to 1994 (Henshaw)
BMW E30 3 Series 1981 to 1994 (Hosier)
BMW GS (Henshaw)
BMW X5 (Saunders)
BMW Z3 Roadster – All models (except M Roadster) 1995 to 2002 (Fishwick)
BSA 350, 441 & 500 Singles – Unit Construction Singles C15, B25, C25, B40, B44 & B50 1958-1973 (Henshaw)
BSA 500 & 650 Twins (Henshaw)
BSA Bantam (Henshaw)
Citroën 2CV (Paxton)
Citroën ID & DS (Heilig & Heilig)
Cobra Replicas (Ayre)
Corvette C2 Sting Ray 1963-1967 (Falconer)
Ducati Bevel Twins (Falloon)
Ducati Desmodue Twins – Pantah, F1, 750 Sport, 600, 750 900 1000 Supersport, ST2, Monster, SportClassic 1979 to 2013 (Falloon)
Ducati Desmoquattro Twins - 851, 888, 916, 996, 998, ST4 1988 to 2004 (Falloon)
Fiat 500 & 600 (Bobbitt)
Fiat Coupé All models 1993 to 2000 (Tipo 175) (Pearson & Vocking)
Ford Capri (Paxton)
Ford Escort Mk1 & Mk2 (Williamson)
Ford Model T – All models 1909 to 1927 (Barker & Tuckett)
Ford Mustang – First Generation 1964 to 1973 (Cook)
Ford Mustang – Fifth generation / S197 2005-2014 (Cook)
Ford RS Cosworth Sierra & Escort – All models 1985-1996 (Williamson)
Harley-Davidson Big Twins – FL, FX/Softail and Dyna series. 1340cc, 1450cc, 1584cc. 1984-2010 (Henshaw)
Ducati 928 (Hemmings)
Hillman Imp – All models of the Hillman Imp, Sunbeam Stiletto, Singer Chamois, Hillman Husky & Commer Imp 1963 to 1976 (Morgan)
Hinckley Triumph triples & fours 750, 900, 955, 1000, 1050, 1200 - 1991-2009 (Henshaw)
Honda CBR FireBlade – 893cc, 918cc, 929cc, 954cc, 998cc, 999cc. 1992-2010 (Henshaw)
Honda CBR600 Hurricane (Henshaw)
Honda SOHC Fours 1969-1984 (Henshaw)
Jaguar E-Type 3.8 & 4.2 litre (Crespin)
Jaguar E-type V12 5.3 litre (Crespin)
Jaguar Mark 1 & 2 (All models including Daimler 2.5-litre V8) 1955 to 1969 (Thorley)
Jaguar New XK 2005-2014 (Thorley)
Jaguar S-Type - 1999 to 2007 (Thorley)
Jaguar X-Type – 2001 to 2009 (Thorley)
Jaguar XJ-S (Crespin)
Jaguar XJ6, XJ8 & XJR – All 2003 to 2009 (X-350) models including Daimler (Thorley)
Jaguar XK 120, 140 & 150 (Thorley)
Jaguar XK8 & XKR (1996-2005) (Thorley)
Jaguar/Daimler XJ 1994-2003 (Crespin)
Jaguar/Daimler XJ6, XJ12 & Sovereign – All Jaguar/Daimler/VDP series I, II & III models 1968 to 1992 (Crespin)
Jaguar/Daimler XJ40 (Crespin)
Kawasaki Z1 & Z900 – 1972 to 1976 (Orritt)
Land Rover Series I, II & IIA (Thurman)
Land Rover Series III (Thurman)
Lotus Seven replicas & Caterham 7: 1973-2013 (Hawkins)
Mazda MX-5 Miata (Mk1 1989-97 & Mk2 98-2001) (Crook)
Mazda RX-8 (Parish)
Mercedes Benz Pagoda 230SL, 250SL & 280SL roadsters & coupés – W113 series Roadsters & Coupes 1963 to 1971 (Bass)
Mercedes-Benz 190 (Parish)
Mercedes-Benz 280-560SL & SLC – W107 series Roadsters & Coupes 1971 to 1989 (Bass)
Mercedes-Benz SL R129-series 1989 to 2001 (Parish)
Mercedes-Benz SLK – R170 series 1996-2004 (Bass)
Mercedes-Benz W123 – All models 1976 to 1986 (Parish)
Mercedes-Benz W124 – All models 1984-1997 (Zoporowski)
MG Midget & A-H Sprite (Horler)
MG TD, TF & TF1500 (Jones)
MGA 1955-1962 (Crosier & Sear)
MGB & MGB GT (Williams)
MGF & MG TF (Hawkins)
Mini (Paxton)
Morris Minor & 1000 (Newell)
Moto Guzzi 2-valve big twins – V7, 850GT, V1000, V7 Sport, 750 S, 750 S3, 850 Le Mans, 1000 Le Mans, 850 T, T3, T4, T5, SP1000, SPII, SPIII, Mille, California, Quota, Strada, California 1100, Sport 1100: 1967-1998 (Falloon)
New Mini (Collins)
Norton Commando (Henshaw)
Peugeot 205 GTI (Blackburn)
Piaggio Scooters – all modern two-stroke & four-stroke automatic models 1991 to 2016 (Willis)
Porsche 911 (964) – Carrera 2, Carrera 4 and turbocharged models. Model years 1989 to 1994 (Streather)
Porsche 911 (993) – Carrera, Carrera 4 and turbocharged models. Model years 1994 to 1998 (Streather)
Porsche 911 (996) – Carrera, Carrera 4 and turbocharged models. Model year 1997 to 2005 (Streather)
Porsche 911 (997) – Model years 2004 to 2009 (Streather)
Porsche 911 (997) – Second generation models 2009 to 2012 (Streather)
Porsche 911 Carrera 3.2 – Coupé, Targa, Cabriolet & Speedster: model years 1984 to 1989 (Streather)
Porsche 911SC – Coupé, Targa, Cabriolet & RS Model years 1978-1983 (Streather)
Porsche 924 - All models 1976 to 1988 (Hodgkins)
Porsche 928 (Hemmings)
Porsche 930 Turbo & 911 (930) Turbo – Coupé. Targa, Cabriolet, classic & slant-nose models: model years 1975 to 1989 (Streather)
Porsche 944 – All models 1982-1991 (Higgins & Mitchell)
Porsche 981 Boxster & Cayman – Model years 2012 to 2016 Boxster, S, GTS & Spyder; Cayman, S, GTS, GT4 & GT4 CS (Streather)
Porsche 986 Boxster – Boxster, Boxster S, Boxster S 550 Spyder: model years 1997 to 2005 (Streather)
Porsche 987 Boxster & Cayman – 1st Generation: model years 2005 to 2009 Boxster, Boxster S, Boxster Spyder, Cayman & Cayman SB (Streather)
Porsche 987 Boxster & Cayman – 2nd generation - Model years 2009 to 2012 Boxster, S, Spyder & Black Editions; Cayman, S, R & Black Editions (Streather)
Rolls-Royce Silver Shadow & Bentley T-Series (Bobbitt)
Royal Enfield Bullet – 350, 500 & 535 Singles, 1977-2015 (Henshaw)
Subaru Impreza (Hobbs)
Sunbeam Alpine – All models 1959 to 1968 (Barker)
Triumph 350 & 500 Twins – 3TA, 5TA Speed Twin, Tiger 90, T100A, T100SS, T100 Tiger, T100S, T100T, T100C, T100R, TR5T, T100D Daytona Series 2 1967 to 1974 (Henshaw)
Triumph Bonneville (Henshaw)
Triumph Stag (Mort & Fox)
Triumph Thunderbird, Trophy & Tiger – 650cc & 750cc models: 1950-1983 (Henshaw)
Triumph TR6 (Williams)
Triumph TR7 & TR8 (Williams)
Velocette 350 & 500 Singles 1946 to 1970 (Henshaw)
Vespa Scooters - Classic 2-stroke models 1960-2008 (Paxton)
Volkswagen Bus (Copping & Cservenka)
Volvo 700/900 Series (Beavis)
VW Beetle (Copping & Cservenka)
VW Golf GTI (Copping & Cservenka)

www.veloce.co.uk

First published in May 2017 by Veloce Publishing Limited, Veloce House, Parkway Farm Business Park, Middle Farm Way, Poundbury, Dorchester, Dorset, DT1 3AR, England.
Fax 01305 250479/e-mail info@veloce.co.uk/web www.veloce.co.uk or www.velocebooks.com.

ISBN: 978-1-845849-91-7 UPC: 6-36847-04991-1

© Chris Barker, Neil Tuckett and Veloce Publishing 2017. All rights reserved. With the exception of quoting brief passages for the purpose of review, no part of this publication may be recorded, reproduced or transmitted by any means, including photocopying, without the written permission of Veloce Publishing Ltd. Throughout this book logos, model names and designations, etc, have been used for the purposes of identification, illustration and decoration. Such names are the property of the trademark holder as this is not an official publication.
Readers with ideas for automotive books, or books on other transport or related hobby subjects, are invited to write to the editorial director of Veloce Publishing at the above address.
British Library Cataloguing in Publication Data – A catalogue record for this book is available from the British Library.
Typesetting, design and page make-up all by Veloce Publishing Ltd on Apple Mac. Printed in India by Imprint Digital (UK).

Introduction & thanks
– the purpose of this book

Fifteen million Model T Fords were built between 1908 and 1927, and Ford dominated the world car market for most of this period. By 1920, more than half the cars on earth were Model Ts. Known in its time as the 'Flivver' or 'Tin Lizzie,' it brought motoring to millions and has justifiably been called 'The Car That Put the World on Wheels;' an international team of journalists voted it 'Car of the (20th) Century.' Nowadays, its basic robustness and reliability, together with excellent availability of cars, parts and knowledge, mean it can be described as 'the 100-year-old car you can still use.' It is one of the few pre-WW2 cars – and probably the only pre-WW1 design – which merits the publication of an Essential Buyer's Guide.

Most Model Ts were made in the USA, but Ford's Canadian factory supplied British Empire territories such as Australia, New Zealand and South Africa, and the Manchester factory built 300,000 Fords for the UK, and supplied parts for assembly plants in Europe.

Owning a Model T Ford means owning a piece of automobile, industrial and social history. It also brings membership of a worldwide community of 'interesting' people.

Model Ts are to be found with all manner of bodies: Touring Cars and Town Cars, Sedans and Speedsters, Taxis and Trucks, Roadsters, and even Railcars and Tractors – but they all share the same engine and transmission, and are built on either the car or the Ton Truck chassis. Many of the bodies were built by Ford; others were aftermarket conversions. This book will help you decide which you want. It also sorts the many Ford myths from the facts. The first myth to deal with is the widespread belief that the Model T was unchanged from 1908 to 1927. In fact, many parts were improved and updated, but are interchangeable, so a car claimed to be built in a given year may be a mixture of components from various years. This book will help you sort them out.

Ford usually introduced changes with 'model years' which, in the USA, began as early as August of the preceding year, and it has proved convenient to apply this rationale to this book. So, a '1917 Ford' refers to one built between August 1916 and July 1917.

Ford justifiably claimed that the Model T was the Universal Car, but it was first an American car, and the majority of Fords and buyers are still to be found in the USA. We have, therefore, mostly used American terms and spellings throughout, with British equivalents following in parenthesis where necessary.

We would like to thank fellow members of the Model T Ford Register of Great Britain (MTFRGB) for their help and support in the production of this book. We also need to thank owners elsewhere, including those in the USA and Australia, who have helped make this book invaluable to all those seeking to buy a Model T. Photographs are the authors' except where otherwise credited.

Chris Barker & Neil Tuckett

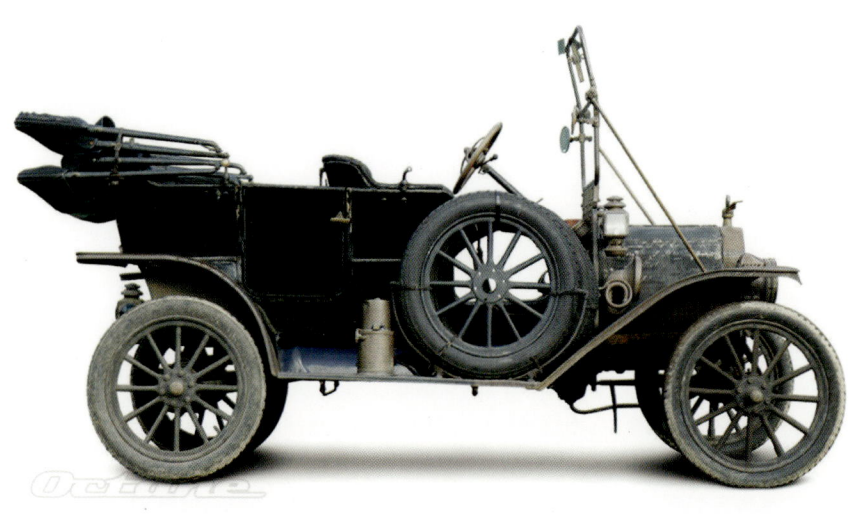

'The 100-year-old car you can still use.' A 1911 Model T Ford Touring Car.
(Courtesy Octane Magazine)

Contents

Introduction & thanks
– the purpose of this book..................3

1 Is it the right car for you?
– marriage guidance............................6

2 Cost considerations
– affordable, or a money pit?..............9

3 Living with a Model T
– will you get along together?...........11

4 Relative values
– which model for you? 14

5 Before you view
– be well informed............................16

6 Inspection equipment
– these items will really help..............19

7 Fifteen minute evaluation
– walk away or stay?.........................21

8 Key points
– where to look for problems 23

9 Serious evaluation
– 60 minutes for years of
enjoyment 24

10 Auctions
– sold! Another way to buy your
dream 43

11 Paperwork
– correct documentation is
essential!..45

12 What's it worth?
– let your head rule your heart! 48

13 Do you really want to restore?
– it'll take longer and cost more
than you think..................................50

14 Paint problems
– bad complexion, including
dimples, pimples and bubbles.........52

15 Problems due to lack of use
– just like their owners, Model Ts
need exercise!..................................53

16 The Community
– key people, organizations and
companies in the Model T Ford
world..55

17 Vital statistics
– essential data at your fingertips.....58

Index..64

The Essential Buyer's Guide™ currency
At the time of publication a BG unit of currency "●" equals approximately US$1.00/£0.82/Euro 0.95. Please adjust to suit current exchange rates using US dollars as the base currency.

1 Is it the right car for you?
– marriage guidance

If you don't think you can live with 35mph cruising, just two forward gears, only rear wheel braking, wooden wheels, the occasional oil drip, and no seat belts or head restraints, then the Model T is probably not for you. But if you want to drive a simple, practical, and robust piece of automotive, social and industrial history, then read on.

The first myth to dispel is that Model Ts are difficult to drive. They are actually very simple; there is no primitive 'crash gearbox' to master, just pedal-operated clutches. It is only a problem for those who are already familiar with modern car controls, but it becomes second nature after the first hundred miles.

Tall and short drivers
Most Model Ts have ample room for all drivers. The exceptions are Town Cars and some Ton Trucks, where payload length took precedence over driver's legroom, and the 1926/27 'Improved' open four-seater Touring Cars and two-seater Roadsters, which have lower seats and are less comfortable for those with long legs.

Weight of controls
Generally medium effort, except for the pre-1926 handbrake, which needs a good pull to make it work. Note that pre-1919 Fords were not supplied with electric starters, and have to be hand-cranked, unless a starter has been added.

Will it fit the garage?
The important parameter may be height: if your garage has a modern 'up-and-over' door which only allows vehicles up to 6ft 6in (1.98m), all but the very last open cars may not fit with the top raised, and early closed Ts and Ton Trucks may not fit at all.

The majority of Model Ts have the 100in wheelbase car chassis. Typical car dimensions are:
- Length 12ft (3.66m)
- Width 5ft 6in (1.68m)

An elegant Town Car (also known as a Landaulette). Driver legroom is sacrificed for room in the back, and it is too high for many modern garages. (Courtesy Chesters, Riley, MTFRGB)

Old or older? Closed or open? Two seats or four? 1926 'Improved' Coupe or 1915 Touring Car?

Ton Trucks (introduced for 1918) have a 124in wheelbase with a heavier chassis and a heavy-duty rear axle
- Typical length 16ft (4.9m)
- Typical width 5ft 8in (1.73m)
- Cab height 7ft (2.13m)

Interior space
All four-seater Model Ts have room for four to five adults. Factory Landaulette (Town Car) and aftermarket 'Depot Hack' bodies can accommodate six. Two-seater cars do not have a rumble (dicky) seat.

Luggage capacity
Four-seater cars' luggage either goes in the rear passenger compartment, or in accessory racks on the rear or on the running boards. Two-seater cars have a separate trunk (boot) – small on most cars, large on 1926-7 models.

Running costs
A gallon of fuel will only take you about 18-22 miles (less if you have a Ton Truck). Tires usually last 5000-10,000 miles and prices are similar to modern tires. Engine oil should be changed at least once per year, but the car requires only the cheapest grade (usually SAE 30).

Usability
Model Ts will go almost anywhere, but a cruising speed of less than 40mph means that high-speed motorways are best avoided. On quieter roads, up to a hundred miles per day is easy, and two hundred is feasible. Those in open cars will need good weatherproof clothing in heavy rain, even with the top raised. Some open cars have sidescreens, but these can restrict visibility. Some DIY skills for everyday maintenance are desirable.

Parts availability
Most Model Ts are in the USA, and most new parts are made by (or for) US specialist suppliers. Owners, clubs and specialists in other countries generally buy parts from US suppliers. Almost everything is available, either as new 'pattern' parts or used.

Parts cost
Not only are parts easily found, but prices are generally among the lowest in the old-car world. Costs are lowest in the USA, the source of most items. Prices elsewhere reflect costs of shipping from the USA and import duties.

Insurance
Specialist classic car insurers will cover all Model Ts at modest cost, usually with an 'agreed value.' One point to bear in mind is that (in the UK, at least) normal policies do not cover commercial hire for weddings, proms, etc.

Investment potential
By the end of the 1920s, the Model T was generally derided; it symbolised the poverty of the Depression. It is only in recent decades that its fundamental virtues have been rediscovered. As the Ford's contemporaries become rarer and harder to restore and maintain, the Model T has found increased favor with those wanting a really old but practical car, and values have increased faster than many other 'classics' – albeit from a low base.

Failings
Whether you have just Ford's original brakes (pedal-operated transmission brake and handbrake on rear drums), or you have extra accessory brakes (such as 'Rocky Mountain'), the Ford's braking is limited by rear tire grip. You will not get better than about 30% efficiency – about the same as a modern car's handbrake – less if it's wet. Driving has to reflect this reality.

If a Model T stops running, the most likely causes are either that the fuel level in the tank under the front seat is too low to go uphill (most 1926-7 Ts have a tank higher up in the scuttle, which eliminates the problem), or there is a fault in the Ford's idiosyncratic ignition system. Owners are well advised to gain some understanding of the system (trembler coils and commutator), or to fit a distributor.

Weatherproof and snug with full sidescreens – not all Touring Cars have them.

Plus points
- Wide availability of cars (and trucks) in all conditions and parts to fix them
- Easy to restore and maintain
- Robust and reliable
- A world-wide community of owners and enthusiasts with all the knowledge and information
- And the Model T raises smiles everywhere

Alternatives
Chevrolets, Dodges, Overlands, Morris Cowley, Austin 7.

2 Cost considerations
– affordable, or a money pit?

The Model T originated in the USA, and the great majority of cars (and almost all new spare parts) are still to be found there. Car prices are usually lower in the USA, and the prices of new US-sourced spare parts bought elsewhere, such as Europe or Australia, are inflated by shipping and duty. The sample list of new spares given in this chapter gives the US$ prices. The same parts in the UK, Australia or New Zealand will cost about 50% more, depending on shipping weight.

Purchase

The usual advice – 'buy the best you can afford' – may not apply here. You may want to restore the car yourself, as Model Ts are not difficult. What is important is that you decide what you want, establish exactly what it is that you are being offered, and that, if it's for you, you pay the right price.

Although Henry Ford stubbornly resisted replacing the Model T for many years, he did apply a 'continuous improvement' policy, and many parts were updated through the 19 years of production. Furthermore, Ford tried to make improved parts interchangeable with old ones, wherever practical. The result today is that an early car is likely to have some later parts – and a late Model T may have early parts. Pre-1917 brass-radiator cars are usually priced higher than later 'black-rad' versions, so it is essential that, if you view a supposed 1916 Ford, you check that it isn't really a 1919 model with an older radiator and a 1926 engine, for example.

There are Model Ts for sale in all conditions. You can buy a bare chassis and collect all the bits; you can buy a running chassis and add a body – maybe make it into a 'Speedster' or 'Depot Hack' – or you can buy a near-perfect restored example. 'Barn find' Fords are still to be found – sometimes untouched for 60 years. The buyer of such a car is faced with a dilemma. The original or 'oily rag' look attracts a lot of attention and has great appeal for many. You fix the mechanical parts and get the car running reliably. But what then? Either you do nothing with the body, or you have to restore absolutely everything; there is really no intermediate course.

Fords built in the UK for that market, and Fords built in Canada for other British Empire territories, were RHD (except for 1919-1921 – because it took two years to solve the problem of the new generator getting in the way of RHD steering!)

'Depot hack' body built from a kit on a post-1917 black radiator chassis on the left; factory 1911 Touring Car with brass radiator on the right.

9

Nowadays, many LHD Model Ts have been imported from the USA into RHD countries. You are not going to be overtaking very often, and the high seat gives excellent visibility, so LHD isn't really a problem.

Spare parts

Spare parts availability for the Model T is astonishingly good. Almost everything you might need is available from about ten US suppliers. The Model T Ford Register of Great Britain (the UK owners' club) maintains a good stock of parts, mostly imported from the USA, for its members. Specialist dealers in the UK and Australia also carry good stocks.

Major items that are not being reproduced, such as chassis frames, axles and engine blocks, are readily available 'used' and can be reconditioned.

Some of the original accessories (non-Ford items) are still being made, notably alternative 'timers' and the Ruckstell and Warford auxiliary gearboxes.

The lists here are a guide to spare parts prices but they vary between suppliers and with time. Prices are from US catalogs in US Dollars and exclude local/country taxes.

New mechanical parts
Cylinder head gasket ●x28
Engine gasket set ●x46
Piston rings set ●x50
Pistons set ●x81
Timing gear ●x54
Flywheel ring gear ●x43
Valve ●x8
Transmission bands set (Kevlar) ●x88
Hose set ●x10
Front spring ●x210
Rear spring ●x390
Spindle (king pin) car set ●x50
Rear brake shoes (lined) ●x81
Exhaust pipe ●x16
Muffler (silencer) ●x41
Rebuilt carburettor ●x110
Carburettor float ●x21

Coil points (set of four pairs) ●x38
Rebuilt generator ●x177
Starter Bendix assembly ●x74
Commutator (timer) ●x68
Crown wheel and pinion ●x332
Axle half shaft ●x90
Ruckstell gearbox ●x2500
Warford gearbox ●x3445
High compression cylinder head ●x380
Radiator (brass, 09-16) ●x1200
Radiator (black, 17-25) ●x800
Tire (front 09-25) ●x180

New body parts
Fender (wing) front ●x525
Fender (wing) rear ●x360
Touring Car top (hood) ●x400
Upholstery kit – Touring Car ●x500

3 Living with a Model T
– will you get along together?

Driving a Model T
Model Ts are not *difficult* to drive, but they are *different*. First impressions can be worrying, but driving becomes second nature after the first hundred miles. The key skill is to look and think ahead to allow for the Ford's limited braking capability.

When you can stop a Model T, you can drive it.
Like today's supercars, the Model T has multiple clutches – one for each gear.
• The left pedal engages low gear if pressed and held down, and high gear if fully released (as long as the handbrake is off). Neutral is halfway.
• The centre pedal engages reverse when pressed and held down.
• The right pedal is the brake.
• The accelerator is a hand control on the steering column.
• The handbrake lever also disengages the high speed clutch to provide a neutral gear.

Low gear is used for starting and for climbing and descending steep hills. Maximum speed in low is about 16mph. High gear is used for most driving, from about 10-42mph.

Once mastered, driving a Model T is very satisfying, but you must expect attention – and usually a smile. The four-cylinder, 2.9-liter engine doesn't usually exceed 1800rpm, but develops 85lb/ft torque at just 1100rpm, so many hills can be climbed at 25-30mph in 'high' gear. You will ascend steep hills in low at 12-15mph. Note: it's good practice to use the same gear while descending steep hills, to make the most of engine-braking. Level road cruising speed is 30-40mph.

One odd feature of Model T ownership is that it's easier to start a cold engine on a cold day with one rear wheel jacked up (see Chapter 9).

Some Model Ts have an auxiliary gearbox. The Ruckstell two-speed axle is the most common. This lowers gearing by one third, giving you a useful ratio filling the gap between normal Ford high and low to climb hills, plus a very, very low gear. The Warford gearbox is a three-speed unit which fits onto the rear

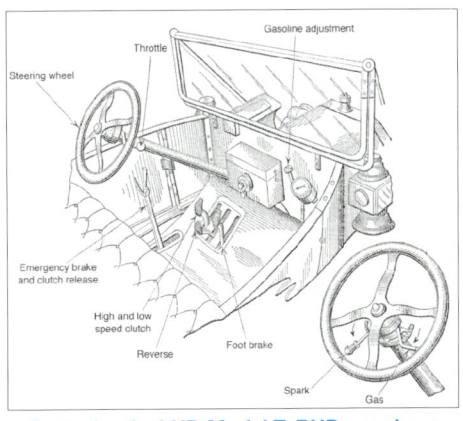

Controls of a LHD Model T: RHD cars have the emergency brake on the driver's right, and the throttle (gas) on the left of the steering column. (Courtesy MTFRGB)

The Ruckstell auxiliary gearbox fits in a special axle casing to the left of the differential. It lowers all gear ratios by 33%.

Rocky Mountain brakes have contracting bands, which work on the outside of rear wheel brake drums. They offload the transmission brake, and are essential for cars with a Warford-type auxiliary gearbox, as, with neutral selected, the transmission brake is separated from the wheels.

The Warford auxiliary gearbox bolts to the rear of the original transmission and requires a shortened driveshaft and torque tube. Most have three ratios – underdrive, direct and overdrive, and therefore provide a total of nine gears, three of them reverse.

Refuelling all but the 'Improved' 1926-7 Model Ts requires the front seat cushion to be lifted out. The low-set fuel tank has to be fairly full for gravity feed to work while ascending steep hills.

of the transmission. It provides neutral, and both overdrive and underdrive ratios, so you get six forward and three reverse gears!

Many Fords have accessory braking systems, usually the 'Rocky Mountain' type, but you can even buy disc brakes. These all work on the rear wheels, so ultimate effectiveness is not improved, but pedal loads are lower and stresses on the transmission are reduced. These brakes are really essential if you have a Warford-type auxiliary gearbox, as, with neutral engaged, the normal transmission brake is disconnected from the rear wheels.

Most open Model Ts have no door on the driver's side, because the handbrake would make access difficult. Both driver and front passenger use the nearside door. Pre-1926 vehicles have the fuel tank under the front seat. The cushion has to be lifted out for refuelling, and the low tank position and gravity feed to the carburettor means that the fuel level has to be kept high if there are steep hills. The scuttle-mounted tank of 1926 'Improved' Fords is much better.

As Model Ts were all built before the introduction of leaded fuel, unleaded fuel is not a problem. Ethanol is not desirable in any old vehicle, but 5% content does not affect running. Ethanol may dislodge paint and other material in the fuel system and cause blockage, and, in the long-term, it may attack rubber, brass and other materials.

Soft-tops are straightforward to erect, but four-seater car tops, especially pre-1923, require two people.

Safety

The Ford dates from an era when road safety was not a great concern. You will not be cocooned in a crash-tested box, surrounded by air-bags and electronics, but your speed will be low and you will probably drive mostly on quiet roads in good weather. There are some sensible measures you can take. Primary safety is improved by fitting turn signals – no-one looks for hand signals today. Even more important, perhaps, is to fit a stop-lamp. We often encounter drivers who fail to use turn signals, but we don't expect vehicles without brake lights. Accidents involving Model Ts are rare, but Fords have been 'rear ended' on fast roads by drivers who were inattentive. It is simple to attach a magnetic reflective strip, or to clip on a bright flashing red LED cycle light, when conditions are poor, or you have to use a fast road. Model T lights, whether gas, oil or electric, are barely adequate for night driving, but can be easily improved, especially with modern LED bulbs, which take little power.

Secondary safety is greatly improved by replacing the original plate glass with modern laminated glass. All the pieces are flat.

Looking after a Model T

The Ford is a simple car. Regular maintenance tasks and checks are very straightforward, and accessibility is excellent. Gaining an understanding of the car's systems (especially the ignition system) is worthwhile and not difficult. The *Ford Service Manual* (available as a reprint) explains everything, advice is freely available, and DVDs covering individual systems have been made. Most owners look after their cars themselves. There is no reason why a competent commercial mechanic should not service your Model T, but many will be reluctant because of lack of familiarity.

'A little and often' is the best approach. Engine oil level should be checked every hundred miles or so. There are about ten points to oil or grease regularly. The oil should be changed, perhaps every 1000 miles, or annually. SAE30 is the usual choice.

It is wise to check the tightness of some important components, such as wooden wheel spokes, rear axle shafts, and steering parts, reasonably often. Cotter pins (split pins) must always be replaced.

If the Model T has its original trembler coil ignition system, then the 'timer' (or 'commutator' – it is really a low-voltage distributor) needs regular cleaning and, depending on the type, lubrication. The coils themselves should be set up with the correct equipment, but should then give no trouble for several years. It is a good idea to carry a spare coil or two.

And there are the famous 'bands.' These are three externally-contracting brakes inside the transmission, each operated by a pedal. One is the main service brake. It acts on the transmission and hence both rear wheels. The other two act as clutches; one engages low gear, the other engages reverse. The bands have a friction material which wears, so they require occasional adjustment. New drivers tend to wear them more rapidly. Adjustment of all three takes about 30 minutes.

Other components tend to be 'on condition;' fix when worn.

Turn signals (indicators) and stop lights are strongly recommended for driving in modern traffic, and need not be obtrusive.

13

4 Relative values
– which model for you?

More buyers look for a four-seater Touring Car than other versions, and many prefer the original brass radiator's appearance, so the datum here (100% value) is a 1915 Touring Car.

The following estimates presume that the vehicles have the correct body and mechanical parts for the claimed year of manufacture. The figures given are only a rough guide – condition is all-important:
- Pre-1915 Touring Cars are worth more than our datum – a 1911 car may be double the price, and earlier ones are higher still
- Black radiator Touring Cars (1917-25) are typically around 80%, and Nickel cars (1926-7) nearer 75%
- Two-seater open cars tend to be worth 10% less than a four-seater of the same year
- The closed 'Centerdoor' (1916-24) may be worth as much as a contemporary Touring version, but later Tudor and Fordor cars (1925-7) are less popular and are at about 60%. Coupes are at about 70% of our datum
- Town Cars (Landaulettes) are rare and may be worth double the price of a Touring Car of the same year

A beautifully-restored 1912 Touring Car. (Courtesy Bob Richmon, Art Gergoudis and MTFCI)

Reduced cost (then and now) and an updated shape for the 1917-on Touring Car. Black radiator and black bodywork. (Courtesy Lilleker Family)

A final style update – the 'Improved' Touring Car for 1926-7 with lowered bodywork, modern tires and nickel-plated radiator. (Courtesy Ford Motor Company and MTFRGB)

The 'Centerdoor' was the first 'sedan' for the family. Stylish, but the center door means that the driver has to fold the passenger's seat for access. Made from 1916 to 1925.

The Tudor two-door sedan appeared in 1925. (Courtesy Roger Florio and MTFRGB)

The rather heavy Fordor four-door sedan appeared in 1925. (Courtesy Lilleker Family)

- Manchester-built vans are liked in the UK and have similar value to a Touring Car of the same year
- Ton Truck values are about 65% of Touring Cars – examples with high or overdrive gears are more sought-after
- Speedsters with stock chassis and engine and minimal bodies start at under 50%. Period bodies, lowered chassis, extra gears and OHV engine conversions increase values considerably
- In the UK, Manchester-built Model Ts have a price premium of about 20%.
- Coachbuilt Fords exist and, if original and good-looking, can be worth much more than factory-bodied cars

   Some accessories affect values:
- An auxiliary gearbox (Ruckstell, Warford) adds about 7%
- Auxiliary rear brakes add about 4%
- A complete period speedometer with cable and drive gears can add about 4%

Coupes and 'Coupelets' were available in various styles, from 1915. This is a 1926 'Improved' car.

Speedsters are popular. Low weight means better performance, and it's an easy solution when you have a running chassis but no body. Some Speedsters have modifications to lower the chassis. The best examples have period engine conversions: an improved side-valve, overhead valve (8- or 16-valve) or even an OHC cylinder head, and maybe a stronger, modified later Model A crankshaft. (Courtesy John Housego)

The UK-designed van, available from 1914. (Courtesy Lilleker Family)

Having seen the success of aftermarket Model T truck conversion kits, Ford introduced its own very successful 'Ton Truck' for 1918.

15

5 Before you view
– be well informed

To avoid a wasted journey, and the disappointment of finding that the car does not match your expectations, it will help if you're very clear about what questions you want to ask, before you pick up the telephone. Some of these points might appear basic, but, when you're excited about the prospect of buying your dream classic, it's amazing how some of the most obvious things slip the mind ... Also check the current values of the model you are interested in in classic car magazines, which give both a price guide and auction results.

Where is the car?
Is it going to be worth traveling to the next county/state, or even across a border? A locally advertised car, although it may not sound very interesting, can add to your knowledge for very little effort, so make a visit – it might even be in better condition than expected.

Dealer or private sale
Establish early on if the car is being sold by its owner or by a trader. A private owner should have all the history, so don't be afraid to ask detailed questions. A dealer may have more limited knowledge of a car's history, but should have some documentation. A dealer may offer a limited warranty/guarantee (ask for a printed copy) and finance.

Cost of collection and delivery
A dealer may well be used to quoting for delivery by car transporter. A private owner may agree to meet you halfway, but only agree to this after you have seen the car at the vendor's address to validate the documents. Conversely, you could meet halfway and agree the sale, but insist on meeting at the vendor's address for the handover.

View – when and where
It is always preferable to view at the vendor's home or business premises. In the case of a private sale, the car's documentation should tally with the vendor's name and address. Arrange to view only in daylight, and avoid a wet day. Most cars look better in poor light or when wet.

Reason for sale
Do make it one of the first questions: why is the car being sold and how long has it been with the current owner? How many previous owners?

Conversions and specials
A Model T with a Ford factory body is always the most straightforward purchase. There are Model Ts with coachbuilt or commercial bodies which were fitted when new, or nearly new. There should be some documentation to support such vehicles' history (old photos, body supplier's advert, etc).

In modern times, many Model T chassis have been rescued, and, in the absence of anything else, fitted with non-standard bodies. The most common are

The 'Depot Hack' was a period aftermarket conversion. Most examples seen today have been built from kits.

Period OHV or even OHC cylinder heads can be very successful, but they are rare and very expensive. Famous names include RAJO, Frontenac ('Fronty'), and Laurel-Roof. (Courtesy Lilleker Family)

Depot Hacks (wooden-bodied, open-sided, roofed commercial vehicles) and Speedsters (often just a hood (bonnet), firewall (scuttle), two seats and a fuel tank). These are less desirable than factory-bodied cars, though Speedsters with OHV conversions, shortened lowered chassis and racing bodies can be worth much more.

It can be claimed that the Model T spawned the car accessory industry, because of Henry Ford's reluctance to add anything, and most Fords have one or more non-standard features. An auxiliary gearbox (usually a Warford or Ruckstell) is, for many, a worthwhile addition, as are extra rear brakes, such as 'Rocky Mountain' ones.

Modifications to improve safety are sensible, even if some originality is lost. These include safety glass, brake and turn lights, electric conversions of oil and gas lights and a speedometer (often a bicycle type – cheap and accurate).

Conversion from LHD to RHD when imported to the UK or Australia, etc, is rare and unnecessary. If it is a pre-1919 vehicle, ask if an electric starter has been fitted.

Condition (body/chassis/interior/mechanicals)
Ask for an honest appraisal of the car's condition. Ask specifically about some of the check items described in Chapter 7. Ask the seller what is *wrong* with the vehicle.

Matching data/legal ownership
Do VIN/chassis, engine numbers and licence plate match the official registration document? Is the owner's name and address recorded in the official registration documents?

For those countries that require an annual test of roadworthiness, does the car have a document showing it complies (or did comply when last tested)?

If a smog/emissions certificate is mandatory, does the car have one?

If required, does the car carry a current road fund license/licence plate tag?

Does the vendor own the car outright? Money might be owed to a finance company or bank: the car could even be stolen. Several organizations will supply the data on ownership, based on the car's license plate number, for a fee. Such companies can often also tell you whether the car has been 'written-off' by an insurance company. In the UK, for example, these organizations can supply vehicle data:

HPI – 01722 422 422,
AA – 0870 316 3564
DVLA – 0300 790 6802
RAC – 0330 159 0364
Most other countries will have similar organizations.

Insurance
Check with your existing insurer before setting out; your current policy might not cover you to drive the car.

How you can pay
A check (cheque) will take several days to clear and the seller may prefer to sell to a cash buyer. However, a banker's draft (a check issued by a bank) is as good as cash, but safer, so contact your own bank and become familiar with the formalities that are necessary to obtain one. An on-line bank transfer may be the best solution, and is increasingly likely to be preferred.

Buying at auction?
If the intention is to buy at auction, see Chapter 10 for further advice.

Professional vehicle check (mechanical examination)
Model Ts are the simplest of vehicles in most respects, but they are *different*. There are some basic checks which should be made. If you feel unsure about making these checks yourself, you may be able to persuade another competent owner to assist (owners' clubs may be able to put you in touch).

There are also organizations that will carry out a general professional check. Contact them via their websites or these numbers:

AA – 0800 056 8040 (motoring organization with vehicle inspectors)
RAC – 0330 159 0720 (motoring organization with vehicle inspectors)
Most other countries will have similar organizations.

6 Inspection equipment
– these items will really help

Before you rush out of the door, gather together a few items that will help as you work your way around the car:

This book
Reading glasses (if you need them for close work)
Magnet (not powerful, a fridge magnet is ideal)
Flashlight (torch)
Probe (a small screwdriver works very well)
Jack
Overalls
Mirror on a stick
Digital or mobile phone camera
A friend, preferably a knowledgeable enthusiast who has Model T driving experience

This book is designed to be your guide at every step, so take it along and use the check boxes to help you assess each area of the car you're interested in. Don't be afraid to let the seller see you using it.

Your inspection kit. You also need someone with Model T driving experience.

Take glasses, if you need them to read documents and make close up inspections.

Rust is rarely a major issue in a Model T, though the lower parts of steel body panels can suffer.

A magnet will help you check if the car has filler, or even has fiberglass panels. Use the magnet to sample bodywork areas all around the car, but be careful not to damage the paintwork. Expect to find a little filler here and there, but not whole panels.

A flashlight (torch) with fresh batteries will be useful for peering under the car.

A small screwdriver can be used – with care – as a probe, particularly on the underside. With this you should be able to check an area of severe corrosion, but be careful – if it's really bad the screwdriver might go right through the metal!

Be prepared to get dirty. Take along a pair of overalls, if you have them. Fixing a mirror at an angle on the end of a stick may seem odd, but you'll probably need it to check the condition of the underside of the car. It and the torch will also help you to peer into some of the important crevices.

The jack is useful for lifting a wheel to check for wear, but you can get under a Model T without raising it.

Use your digital or mobile phone camera; take photos so that, later, you can study some areas of the car more closely. Take a picture of any part of the car that causes you concern, and seek a friend's opinion.

A smartphone app or a hand-held GPS is useful to measure speed accurately, especially if the vehicle has no speedometer.

Ideally, have a friend or knowledgeable enthusiast accompany you: a second opinion is always valuable. You will need someone – your friend or the seller – who has experience of driving a Model T.

7 Fifteen minute evaluation
– walk away or stay?

The priorities are to establish exactly what you are viewing – year, model, etc – whether it's the sort of Ford you want, and whether it's in a condition that makes it worth inspecting more closely.

The myth is that Henry Ford refused to change the Model T over its 19-year production life. It's true that he held out against replacement, but he *did* change many parts – and as new parts were often designed to be interchangeable with old ones, it's possible to have a vehicle with parts of all ages.

Note that Ford's model years usually started in August of the previous year, so production of 1917 cars began in August 1916. References in this book follow the same convention.

The first guide to date will be the appearance – notably the radiator. 1908-1916 cars had the distinctive brass radiator; then came radiators with black-painted pressed-steel shells. These were increased in height by 1.4in for 1924. Finally, there were nickel-plated radiator shells for 1926 (though commercials usually still had black). Under the skin, the chassis should be the basis for dating. All engines had numbers, but, until December 1925, chassis were not numbered. Chapter 9 shows you how to identify different chassis and engines. A car with a wooden firewall (pre-1923) may have a serial number plate on it.

Ask about or check for modifications, such as an auxiliary gearbox or extra brakes. Also check to see if a pre-1919 Model T has had an electric starter, and perhaps a generator, added. These changes are fairly common, especially when aging owners find that they can no longer hand-crank cars into life. This may even be a consideration for you …

If you are viewing a Ton Truck, it is important to determine whether it has the lowest axle ratio (which limits cruise speed to below 25mph), the higher factory gearing (30mph) or, best of all, an extra overdrive gearbox.

You may also find luggage, fuel or spare wheel racks, extra horns or even a period speedometer (not factory-fitted after mid-1914). Check whether the original ignition system of timer and four trembler coils is still fitted, or has been replaced by a distributor, HT magneto or a 'True-Fire' (a modern device which replaces the trembler coils and timer).

Ask which parts have been replaced or restored during the seller's ownership, and ask if there are any spares to be sold with the vehicle.

Check for basic extra safety features: turn and brake lights, electrified oil or gas lamps, and safety glass.

It's important to find out some recent history. Unless you are looking for a restoration project, a car or truck that has been driven and used regularly by an enthusiastic owner is the best and safest choice. It's good to find a Ford that has had a fairly recent independent roadworthiness check. The UK's 'MoT Test'

The brass radiator was used from 1908 to late 1916. (Courtesy Bob Richmon, Art Gergoudis and MTFCI)

21

is no longer compulsory, but some sensible owners submit vehicles for test anyway, every few years. Vehicles imported from places with no official tests have often been found to have alarming faults. Beware, also, of vehicles that have come from museums or 'collections.' They have often not been used, and have sometimes only been 'restored' to look good.

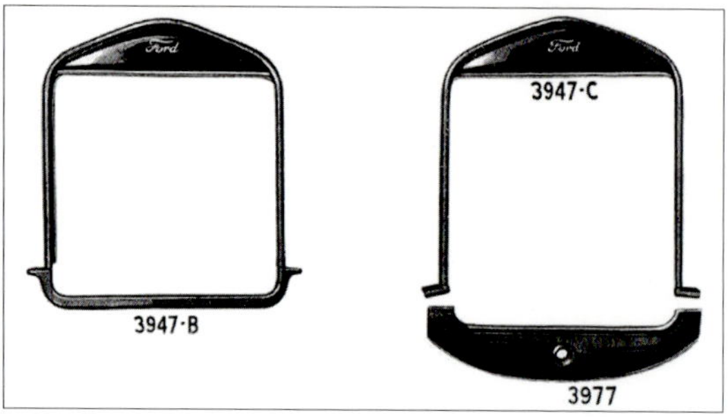

If you are keen, or at least prepared to do work yourself, then a car with no recent usage can still be a good buy *at the right price,* as restoration of a Model T is much easier than for most newer cars.

The 'low' black radiator with painted steel shell, of 1917 to late 1924, and the later 'high' version, initially black but then nickel-plated for the 'Improved' 1926-7 Fords. (Courtesy Ford Motor Company and MTFRGB)

There are a few useful checks to start with. If the Ford has factory wheels with wooden spokes, tap the spokes to see if any are loose, and then pull and push the top of each tire sideways. If the wheel creaks or flexes noticeably, repairs will be needed. Brown rust dust is often evidence of a problem.

Jack up each rear wheel in turn and check for up-and-down or axial play. Anything more than 'perceptible' could mean a rear axle rebuild. Check the brake drums for oil leaks.

Perform similar checks on the front axle, looking for wear in wheel bearings, trackrod ends or spindles (kingpins). Also check that free rotational play at the steering wheel rim is no more than about 2in (50mm).

Check tires – not just tread depth, but also sidewalls for cracking; Model Ts are still found with 1920s tires!

Check over the body and trim. You can easily remove the floorboards and seat cushions to see more. If it's an open vehicle, erect and lower the top (pre-1923 Touring cars need two people for this), checking hood 'bows' and fabric. The fabric may have shrunk. Perhaps most importantly, think about whether it has the body style you want. Will its height fit your garage?

Unless you have already rejected the vehicle, ask the seller to start it. This process should tell you quite a lot about both Ford and owner. If it runs fairly smoothly, a short test run is next. This should be performed by a driver with experience – ideally your knowledgeable 'friend,' but perhaps the owner. If it's your first ride in a Model T, you won't know what to expect, but the car should pull away and then, after engaging high gear, it should gather speed to cruise at 30-35mph on a level road. It should also be free of jerks down to about 10mph in high. Expect low and reverse gears to be audible. If allowable, a brake test which locks the rear wheels is reassuring.

Simple checks can tell you a lot. (Courtesy MTFRGB)

8 Key points
– where to look for problems

- Exactly what is it? Are the key components consistent with the claimed date of manufacture?
- Does the official paperwork – registration document (eg USA title, or UK's V5), import documents, etc – match the actual vehicle? And is it adequate to allow usage in your country, state, etc?
- Ownership history: few owners and long-term ownership are good. History and photos of work done are desirable. Be wary if there have been lots of recent owners and documentation is sparse
- Does the Model T have a Ford factory body? If not, is the body 'period' or recent? Is it the type you really want? Will it fit your garage (including height)?
- What non-standard features are there (auxiliary gearbox or brakes, different ignition system, upgraded or additional lights, speedometer, racks etc)? Are they desirable, tolerable or removable?
- What documentary evidence is there that the Ford is roadworthy? Recent extensive usage (at least a hundred miles/year) is good. Independent test documentation (eg UK 'MoT' test certificates) under three years old is reassuring.
- Do physical checks of wheels, tires, axles, steering, suspension, split pin use, fluid leaks, etc, support roadworthiness claims?
- Does the vehicle start and run in all gears, and does it stop?
- Is the bodywork, paint and trim (seats, top/hood, linings, etc) in good condtion?

Coachbuilt cars are rare, but can be very attractive. A striking appearance, with all the practicality of the factory vehicle. (Courtesy N Georgano)

23

9 Serious evaluation
– 60 minutes for years of enjoyment

You will be buying a Model T Ford because you want one; certainly not because it fits your transport needs, and, if you examine several Fords, as you should, it's hard to remember the exact details of each. This chapter tries to bring some objectivity to this unreliable, subjective and emotional process. Not only will it help you decide *which* car (or commercial) to buy, it can also help you identify 'bargaining points' when it comes to pricing. The sections are specifically tailored to the Model T – their particular weaknesses and the differences between years. **As you will probably not be familiar with the Model T Ford, each section describes what to expect as well as what to check.** Mark (or ask your friend to mark) each section Excellent (4), Good (3), Average (2), or Poor (1), being as realistic as possible. Use your magnet and small probe when checking for rust. You can inspect most parts of the underside without recourse to a jack or stands – you only need a jack to lift a wheel.

A note about very early cars
The Model T was launched in late 1908. In the first two years of production there were several significant design changes and many minor ones. Early engines had exposed valves, the first 2500 had a water pump and, initially, there were two levers and two pedals to control the gears. Early rear axle casings were cleverly made, but weak. Only 14,000 cars (0.1% of total production) were produced up to the end of 1909, and only 21,000 during 1910. Survivors are rare and very expensive. If you are contemplating buying an early Model T, it is vital to ensure that it is genuine. Expert help – or at least close study of Bruce McCalley's book *Model T Ford, The Car that Changed the World* – is recommended.

General appearance and fit   [4] [3] [2] [1]
Look carefully at the vehicle from each side, then from the front and rear. Does it 'sit' well? Do the hood and doors fit? Is the car level when viewed from behind?

Model year   [4] [3] [2] [1]
Is the Ford's year the one claimed? Does it have the right parts?

The main year identifiers are the radiator, engine block, chassis and body. Check these individually, as described below, then come back to score this one. Remember that the Ford model year began in the preceding August.

Original parts are harder to find for early cars, such as this very original 1911.

Ton Truck rear wheels with detachable rims have six bolts (cars have four).

This wheel has woodworm in the spokes and felloes, rust in the rim, and cracks in the tire sidewalls!

Wheels

Most Model Ts have spokes made from wood (shagbark hickory, which is superior to oak or ash). Prior to 1918, the felloes (inner part of the wheel rim) were also wood. Spokes must be sound and free of woodworm. Look for brown rust dust and check for loose spokes by tapping them. One or two loose spokes, but no more, can be shimmed at their outer ends. Also check each complete wheel, by pushing and pulling sideways on the top of the tire. If there are 'creaks' or observable movement, repairs are essential. Lateral run-out can be checked when the vehicle is jacked up (see below).

Check that all four wheels are the same type.

From 1919, Ford supplied wheels with detachable *rims*. Earlier cars, especially in the UK, may have detachable *wheel* accessory conversions.

Some 'Improved' cars, especially those made in 1927, have wire wheels with welded spokes.

Tires (tyres)

Until the introduction of the 'Improved' Fords in late 1925, Model T cars were fitted with clincher (beaded edge) rims and tires, which *must* be run at 50-60lb/in^2 or they are liable to come off the rims.

Check the tire sizes. Rear clincher tires are 30 x 3.5in, and most fronts are 30 x 3in. The first figure is the *outside* diameter; the second is the width. As tire width is almost the same as height, the front wheel rims are slightly larger than the rears (24in versus 23in).

Confusingly, 1911 to 1913 UK-built Model Ts had metric wheels and tires, with 760 x 90mm rears and 750 x 85mm fronts (approx 22in rim diameter).

'Improved' Ford cars have

Many Ton Trucks were fitted with solid or 'drilled solid' rear tires.

Pre-1919 radius rods connected to the 'perches' above the front axle (arrowed).

1919-27 radius rods bolted under the axle (arrowed) to prevent the axle folding under in an accident. The axle MUST be tilted rearwards.

UK 'dropframe' Fords were supplied by Manchester from 1924. The front axle was swept upwards at its ends, the radius rods were moved to the top of the axle, and the rear spring was housed in a deeper rear crossmember.

conventional tires sized as for modern tires, usually 4.50 x 21 – where '21' is the *wheel* diameter in inches. These are run at about 30lb/in^2. 'Improved' car wooden wheels have detachable split rims with a bolted joint, allowing them to be collapsed slightly (with a special tool) for tire fitting and removal. For 1927, wire wheels with welded spokes and a normal 'well-base' were common.

Ton Trucks have 30 x 3.5in front tires and typically 32 x 4.5in (or 6.00 x 20in) rears – but some vehicles have solid or 'drilled solid' rear tires.

Whatever the tires, they must not only have legal tread depth, but also be free of serious sidewall cracks. Fords are still occasionally 'found' with prewar tires! Look closely where the sidewall meets the 'clincher' rim's edge – this is the most common failure point.

Front axle and steering   [1]

First, have a general look. Early cars' radius rods were attached to the *top* of the axle; from 1919, they bolt underneath (except for UK 'Dropframe' vehicles from 1924).

It is vital that the front axle is mounted so that it tilts *backwards*, but it is possible to misassemble it to tilt *forwards,* which is dangerous as the steering will try to go to full lock. Check that any centering 'dimple' on the top of each perch is to the *rear*. Jack each end of the axle in turn. Check for wear in the spindle, by trying to rock the top of the wheel in and out. This check will also show wheel bearing free play – it should be just noticeable. All Fords have conventional bearing adjustment. From 1919, the original ball bearings were superseded by taper roller bearings. Many earlier cars have been converted. Spin each wheel to check run-out. Expect up to about 0.4in laterally at the tire tread.

Check for trackrod end and drag link wear by attempting to 'steer' each wheel.

Check rotational play in the steering wheel; it should be no more than 2in. If excessive, try to determine whether the wear is in the tiny gearbox in the steering wheel hub, or in the bottom bearing, drag link, trackrod, etc.

Replacement spindles and trackrod end bolts are not expensive.

Try, also, to 'rock' the steering wheel: it sits on a very short shaft and the bearings can wear.

With all these checks, don't expect perfection, but take note of excessive wear.

Rear axle and brakes

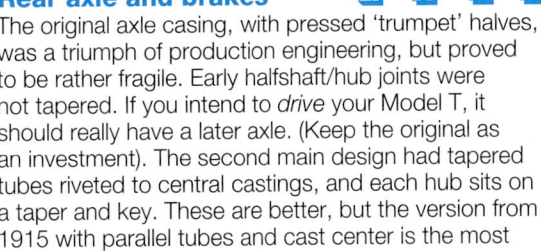

The original axle casing, with pressed 'trumpet' halves, was a triumph of production engineering, but proved to be rather fragile. Early halfshaft/hub joints were not tapered. If you intend to *drive* your Model T, it should really have a later axle. (Keep the original as an investment). The second main design had tapered tubes riveted to central castings, and each hub sits on a taper and key. These are better, but the version from 1915 with parallel tubes and cast center is the most durable.

Lateral loads are taken by a thrust washer each side of the differential. Original washers had 'babbitt' bearing material, but modern bronze is much better. Two checks are recommended. First jack up each wheel in turn (handbrake off, other wheels chocked) and check for free play up-and-down and in-and-out. Don't expect perfection. Excessive vertical freedom may just require a new sleeve for the outer bearing, but the halfshaft may also be worn. Significant in-and-out freedom means an axle rebuild. The second check is to try to sample the axle oil (via the filler plug on the right of the center casting). If it is silvery, there are (or were recently) babbitt thrust washers. These should be replaced without delay.

Axle noises – excessive whine or 'clonks' – should be assessed during the road test.

A rear axle rebuild is messy but not difficult, but it is much better and cheaper to do it *before* something breaks.

Check the bottom of each brake backplate for significant oil leaks. Cars before late 1925 'Improved' vehicles had small (8in diameter) drums with *unlined* iron shoes. Many cars now have lined shoes, which improve the poor performance a little – ask about this. 'Improved' cars have larger, 11in drums with lined shoes, and these are very effective.

Look for auxiliary rear brakes; usually the 'Rocky Mountain' contracting band type, but sometimes modern discs. These offload the transmission and, if a Warford-type gearbox has been added, ensure that you have brakes if neutral is engaged.

Check that the pawl and ratchet of the handbrake works properly.

Ton Trucks have a completely different, heavier axle with worm final drive. You can perform checks as

The first Model T axle casings were formed of just two very deep pressings. This is the next (1911) version with tapered tubes riveted to cast centre halves.

Large washers take all lateral loads in the rear axle. Originally, these had white metal thrust faces, but they should be replaced by modern bronze washers.

Rear drum brakes were 8in diameter and unlined until late 1925. Most cars now have lined shoes.

27

The larger 11in brakes of the 1926-7 cars are much more effective.

above, but the most important check is to determine the ratio. Two were used, 7.25:1 and 5.17:1. Both are low, but the lower ratio really restricts speed to below 25mph, unless an auxiliary overdrive gearbox has been fitted. For serious driving on the road, the 5.17:1 worm, or an overdrive box – and preferably both – are needed.

Radiator [4] [3] [2] [1]

The brass radiator was used from the start of production in late 1908 to late 1916, when it was replaced by the 'low' black radiator, which has a separate black-painted steel shell. The 'high' radiator (the core is 18.4in (467mm) high instead of 17in (432mm)), became standard in late 1923. High radiators have a splash apron below the radiator around the crank handle. 'Improved' Fords, introduced in late 1925, usually had nickel-plated radiators (commercials and some of the cheapest cars stayed with black). The UK got the nickel radiator earlier, in 1923. Note that chromium plating did not appear until about 1928 and so was never used on Model Ts.

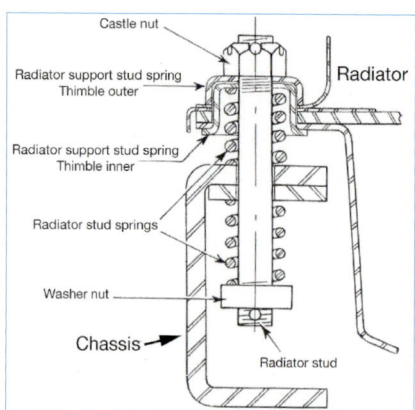

From 1919, the radiator is isolated from chassis flexing by springs in its side mounting bolts. Early cars had a leather pad in place of the upper spring. (Courtesy Ford Motor Co and MTFRGB)

Radiators were originally round-tube construction, but most surviving Fords now have a conventional oval-tube-and-fin core. Check for leaks. The system is not pressurized. If over-filled, water will spill via the overflow pipe on the left side. Check the hose connection castings; they can corrode away. Check also that the side mounting bolts for the radiator have springs which allow flexing.

Engine [4] [3] [2] [1]

Very early engines had a number between the center exhaust ports, then, later, behind the cam gear housing. From 1912, Ford stamped the engine number just above the water inlet on the left side. See Chapter 17 for year and other data. Until late 1925, this was the *only* useful number on the car. (Note that there may be a body number applied by the body supplier elsewhere, and some cars have a serial number on the firewall.)

There are four main engine block types:
• 1908-11: open valve blocks, and the first 2500 cars had a water pump
• 1911-22: valves have two-piece covers (one-piece thereafter)

An early engine with exposed valves and springs.

28

1911 valves have two covers; no provision for a generator.

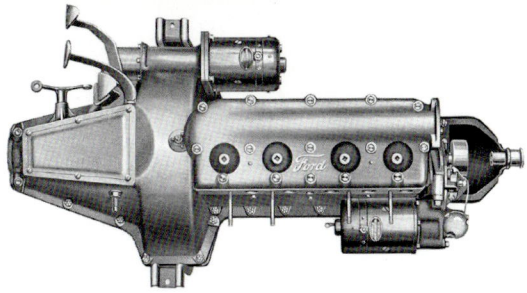

1919-27 engine blocks have a mounting pad for the 6v generator on the front right side, and a starter motor mounted on the left side of the transmission housing. (Courtesy Ford Motor Co and MTFRGB)

• 1919-27: the block and timing cover have provision for mounting the generator on the front right side
• 1925-27: the block has a pair of cast lugs on the back face, near the top, with tapped holes to allow the transmission cover ('hog's head') to be bolted to it. The valve cover is one-piece, and most were not pierced for the throttle linkage

There are two-cylinder head types. The 'low' variety was used until late 1916. The subsequent 'high' head is so named because its top face is higher, to provide more water volume. However, the 'high' head has a lower compression ratio, and hence a little less power. Good 'low' heads are becoming rare. High-compression accessory heads are still made – the aluminum 'Z Head,' which works well, is the most common. OHV and even OHC conversions (eg RAJO, Frontenac) were made in the Model T era. These can work very well, but are now very rare and expensive. It is worth seeking expert advice before buying. Most heads take ½in BSP tapered-thread sparkplugs, but UK heads from 1911 to 1913 had 18mm parallel-thread plugs.

'Improved' 1926-7 engine blocks have a one-piece valve cover and two cast lugs on the rear to attach the transmission cover (hog's head) and lateral support straps. Clutch and brake pedals are wider, too.

The original 'low' cylinder head, used until late 1916.

The 1917-27 'high' cylinder head, with greater water volume, but a lower compression ratio (4:1 instead of 4.5:1). Height at the bolts is about 2.7in (69mm) – the low head height is about 2.1in (53mm).

Fords were supplied with two taps to check oil level. Here, the lower tap has been replaced by an accessory sight glass, which shows exactly where the level is before starting – but, if it isn't empty when the engine runs, it is blocked or stained.

Check for cracks and repairs. Expect minor oil leaks, usually from the rear at each side where block, hog's head and pan meet, and perhaps from the front of the crankshaft.

The Model T has a strange and somewhat illogical system for checking oil level. There are two taps in the right side of the crankcase, just behind the flywheel. The oil level is supposed to be above the lower tap level, and below the upper. With a rag or cup to catch oil, *briefly* open the lower tap. Oil should flow. Then open the upper tap. If a little oil flows, the level is safe. There are accessories to improve the system. Dip-stick conversions have been made, but the most common accessory is a sight glass in place of the lower tap. These are fine as long as you check not only that there is oil present with the engine stopped, but also that oil is *not* present in the glass with the engine running – this shows that the glass is not blocked or stained. Ford fitted no oil (or air) filter.

'Improved' (1926-7) Fords' cooling fans are hung from the water outlet casting – earlier cars had brackets on the timing cover. Accessory water pumps were – and still are – made. However, most owners agree that a pump is neither needed nor desirable. If one is fitted, ask why. It may be masking some basic problem.

Transmission

There are really just two types, but there were several designs of the upper cover, known as the 'hog's head,' in the early years. Until late 1915, the hog's head was made of aluminum; it was iron thereafter. Most notably, post-1919 hog's heads have provision for a starter motor. These covers are often fitted to earlier cars (along with a

The Model T's famous 'bands' are forced by the pedals into contact with these spinning drums. The front pair act as clutches for low and reverse gears; the rear one is the transmission brake. This 1926 Ford has the wider brake band.

An 'Improved' Model T band. It has one detachable ear, allowing it to be changed without removing the hog's head.

A 1919-25 LHD hogshead. The starter mounts on the left at the front. Its Bendix mechanism is covered by a cap on the rear (this side). Note narrow pedals. (Courtesy Steve Jelf)

Post-1919 RHD hog's heads with the pedals are on the right. The 'Improved' 1926 version on the right has two lugs which bolt to the rear of the engine block. The central panel allows access to the bands.

flywheel ring gear) to provide electric start.

Prior to the 'Improved' Fords from late 1925, the pedals are narrow, and all three 'bands' (the friction clutches inside the transmission) are identical. 'Improved' Fords have wider left and right pedals, the brake band inside the transmission is wider than the other two, and the 'hog's head' has a pair of lugs at the top, which bolt to the rear of the block. Check that these lugs are braced by steel strips to the frame at the sides.

Expect to see minor oil leaks from the pedal shafts and the driveshaft joint. Ask if there is an oil screen – a common and very useful accessory – under the access cover.

Many Model Ts have had accessory auxiliary gearboxes fitted, usually the Ruckstell 'two-speed-axle' which has gears alongside the differential to lower the gearing by 33%, or the Warford type which bolts onto the rear of the Ford transmission and requires shortened driveshaft, torque tube and radius arms. Warford boxes have both overdrive and underdrive ratios and neutral.

The only significant useful check is to drive and operate the vehicle.

Engine/transmission crankcase (oil pan)

This large pressing forms the sump and the lower casing for the transmission and incorporates the three mounts for the whole engine/transmission assembly (which weighs 470lb (213kg)). There are 'ears' alongside the flywheel cover which bolt to the chassis, and a tubular mounting around the crank handle at the front. All but pre-1911 cars have a detachable cover below the crankshaft. 'Improved' Fords have a large 'four-dip' cover; prior to this, there was a shorter 'three-dip'cover under cylinders one to three.

Check the whole crankcase for signs of damage – dents, bends, recent welding. Brazing *may* date from original manufacture. Check, especially, the side mounting ears for signs of repairs – or existing cracks Also check the rear mounting and spherical bearing for the front radius rods.

All Model Ts were supplied with 'splash pans' – a simple steel pressing each side of the engine, linking the side of the block to the underside of the chassis frame. They

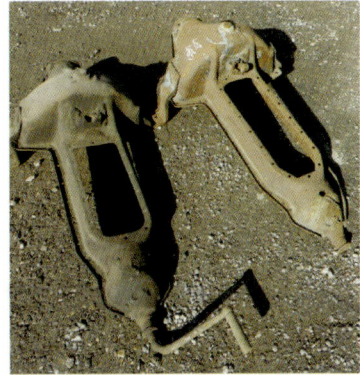

Model T crankcases/oil pans (shown inverted). They carry the engine and transmission and attach to the chassis at the sides and front. 1926 cars have a longer 'four-dip' access cover (right).

were intended to reduce dust and mud ingress. Most have been discarded or lost over the years, so their presence may indicate a particularly well cared for or well restored vehicle.

Ignition system ④ ③ ② ①

This deserves its own section in this chapter as its operation is crucial to both performance and reliability. The 'stock' system uses four trembler coils powered by the flywheel 'magneto' (which is actually an alternator producing up to 30v AC), and controlled by the 'commutator' or 'timer' – and the driver's hand lever. The timer is mounted on the front end of the camshaft.

This system performs well, as long as all the components are in good condition and properly maintained. The timer requires regular attention – cleaning and, if it's the original roller type, frequent oiling. The coils can be adjusted to work using a simple tester, but perform best when set up with special equipment. Once set up, they work well for several years. The magneto output can deteriorate (often restorable by in-car re-magnetizing), or fail entirely. With no magneto, the Model T will run quite well using 12v DC; less well on the original 6v system.

If the Ford has the stock system, ask what type of timer is fitted, and when. There are several types still being made. Also ask who set up the coils, and when. Ask if the sale includes spare coils – wise owners carry one or two.

Pre-1926 cars have the coil box mounted on the rear of the firewall, above the transmission. 'Improved' Fords have the box bolted to the left and above the cylinder head. Check that the box has a lid which fits well – it holds the coils in place. You may find wood or card packers used to keep coils in contact. Pre-1914 coils, and hence their box, varied in design, and are not interchangeable with later coils.

Owners who have lost trust in the coils may fit the 'True-Fire.' This is a physical and functional replacement for the four coils and timer, using modern electronics. It runs on 12v (the latest units also work on 6v).

High tension magneto ignition is a more radical option – but these kits were available in period.

The magneto's stator bolted to the rear of the engine.

Magnets on the front of the flywheel spin close to the magneto's coils.

The commutator or timer mounts on the front end of the camshaft, and acts as a low-voltage distributor to switch the trembler coils. Aftermarket brush or flapper designs are common alternatives to this Ford roller type.

Coil boxes were originally wood; later mostly metal. The lid must be present, as it holds the four individual coils in place and in contact. Note the narrow pedals. (Courtesy Bob Richmon, Art Gergoudis and MTFCI)

1926-7 coil boxes were mounted on the top of the engine. This is how you prevent cylinders two and three firing, in order to check one and four.

They generally work well, or not at all. A rebuild is difficult and, hence, expensive.

The most common alternative ignition system is the conventional distributor – kits are still made today. This replaces the whole Ford system, the distributor being driven off the front of the camshaft in place of the timer.

With the factory system, be sure to confirm that the engine runs when switched to 'mag.' (The ignition switch or key turns anti-clockwise for 'bat' and clockwise for 'mag.') If it only runs on 'bat,' the magneto is not working. Sometimes, the magneto is removed, perhaps to reduce the effective flywheel inertia in a Speedster, or after the violent loss of one or more magnets. The magnets have an important secondary function, which is to throw oil up into a funnel, that then directs it to the front bearings. If the magnets are removed, oil-throwing vanes must be bolted in their place.

Having determined what is fitted – and whether it works, you must decide if it's what you want.

Many people regard the Ford coils and timer as a fundamental part of the Model T's character. You can change the system, but should allow for the cost.

Repair of the magneto (except for in-car re-magnetizing) means removing the engine, and then separating the transmission and flywheel. If the magneto has previously been removed entirely, you will have to find a used set of 16 magnets, bolts and clamps and a stator: it will be prudent to have the stator rewound and the magnets re-charged before installation.

Electrical system

All Model Ts have the ignition system described above. In addition, there are three possibilities – nothing, 6v or 12v.

For 1919, the 6v system – battery, starter and generator – was added. This powered the horn, headlamps, a single tail lamp and, from late 1925, an optional brake lamp. The magneto was retained for ignition, but the battery powered the ignition for starting. Adding just a battery to an early car makes hand-crank starting much easier.

Properly maintained – and with the correct heavy-gauge battery/starter cables – the 6v system is adequate, but many owners convert to 12v. The generator and starter can be modified correctly for 12v, but most owners just change the battery and bulbs and adjust the generator. 12v batteries are cheaper, adding turn signals and lighting is easier with 12v, and starting is much improved, but the Bendix mechanism has a harder life.

Pre-1919 Fords can be converted for electric start by changing the hog's head and flywheel and adding a starter motor. It isn't possible to add the Ford generator to these engines, but there are modern belt-drive add-on alternator kits available. There are also kits which make the magneto charge the battery.

It is important to find out what is fitted to the car and whether it works. The ammeter will show whether the generator is charging (5A to 10A at normal running speed).

Check the wiring quality. With good, simple-to-fit replacement looms available at very modest cost, there is no reason to have messy, heavily modified or dangerous wiring.

Opinions of battery master switches differ. They prevent other faults, such as a stuck generator cut-out causing damage or a fire, but many are poor quality and reduce the voltage at the starter motor. If the battery is disconnected while running, the generator wiring may melt. If you buy a car without a master switch, it is a good idea to disconnect the battery when not in use, at least until you have confidence in the electrical system.

Early cars have gas (acetylene) headlamps and oil side and tail lights. (Courtesy Bob Richmon, Art Gergoudis and MTFCI)

Electric headlamps appeared during 1915.

Lights

Purists can still make the original oil lamps on the firewall and tail work (though they can 'blow out'). Gas headlamps can work well, but they require careful attention, and the carbide fuel is potentially hazardous.

Fords made before 1914 had just oil and gas lamps. During 1915, electric headlamps were fitted; these (and a horn) were powered by the flywheel magneto. They had 9v bulbs wired in series, and brightness varied with engine speed. With the introduction of the generator in 1919, conventional 6v headlamp bulbs were fitted. Oil sidelamps were retained until 1923, but from 1921 UK vehicles also had electric sidelamps.

Most Model Ts now have some sort of electric light conversion. Specific kits are available, but LED cycle lamps are useful – some fit inside the oil lamp bodies. LEDs are a welcome development for old car owners because they use very little power and are cheap and small. LED replacement 'bulbs' are available as direct replacements for most filament bulb types.

Whatever lights are fitted, they should work, but don't expect the electric headlamps to be much use, unless fitted with expensive LED bulbs.

Find out exactly what is fitted and whether it works. Also look at the wiring and hardware installation: it should be neat – and safe.

Fuel system

The system is very simple; just a tank with a sediment trap (with gauze filter) and on-off tap feeding a carburettor by gravity. 'Improved' cars from late 1925 (except the Fordor) have the tank in the scuttle. Other Model Ts have the tank under the front seat and, for ascending steep hills, the fuel level needs to be kept high.

Check the outside of the tank for corrosion, and try to look at the inside, using a torch, to assess corrosion and 'silt.' Check that the tap (and/or any additional non-original tap) works and does not leak. Factory Fords had metal pipes, but some vehicles now have rubber or plastic, which may be attacked by ethanol in modern fuel. Plan to replace rubber or plastic with metal. An in-line paper filter should not be necessary, and can impair gravity-flow feed.

Ford used various carburettors, but NH (introduced for 1920), Kingston and Holley are most common. 1926-7 vehicles usually have a 'Vaporizer' – designed to cope with poor quality fuel.

The carburettor is mounted low down so that gravity fuel feed can work. (Courtesy Bob Richmon, Art Gergoudis and the MTFCI)

Designed to manage with the very poor quality fuel then sold in the USA, the 1926-7 Vaporizer passes fuel through a chamber which is heated by the exhaust.

Check the fuel system for signs of leaks. Modern fuels containing ethanol are not kind to old car systems and many materials, but Fords do not need lead replacement additives.

Chassis and underside

In addition to checks of the engine, transmission, rear axle and suspension described elsewhere, check the chassis frame for excessive rust, loose rivets and physical damage. Early cars have forged brackets to support the body and fenders (wings). A longer rear crossmember from May 1913 eliminated the need for forged

A pile of Model T chassis, rear view. From the top they are:
1) Ton Truck
2) 1913-1920 with forged running board brackets
3) 1921-25
4) 1926-27
5) 1924-25 UK dropframe
6) 1926-27 UK dropframe

35

rear body brackets. 'Improved' cars from late 1925 have a much longer rear crossmember to support the new bodies. UK 'Dropframe' cars from 1924 have a higher bulge over the rear spring. All chassis components were riveted together. Check for loose or missing rivets. Look along the frame for signs of sagging. An ill-fitting hood (bonnet) may also indicate sagging.

Battery carrier on the left and exhaust on the right, in front of this later rear axle.

Check for broken leaves in the front and rear springs and that the spring clamps are sound. The springs should really be oiled or greased.

'Improved' Fords from the end of 1925 have the engine number stamped on the top of the chassis on the right, below the front floor boards.

If the car has a battery carrier on the left in front of the rear axle, check its frame and the adjacent chassis for corrosion. Check the cross-pieces which support the running boards and fenders. From 1920, the original forged running-board brackets were replaced by pressings.

Model T floors were all made of wooden planks set across the car. There should be steel finishers around the slots for the handbrake and pedals, and perhaps a steel draft deflector below the pedals under the boards. Rotten boards should have been replaced with traditional materials.

Exhaust

The system is very simple. There should be a cylindrical muffler (silencer) in front of the rear axle. Early cars had a tail pipe and an asbestos wrap, both discontinued by 1917. Cast iron end caps were replaced by steel pressings from 1921. A simple pipe slides into the front of the silencer and is attached to the manifold by a large brass nut. Check that this connection, particularly its thread on the manifold, is secure. RHD cars have a different shape pipe to clear the pedals. A modern silencer is neither necessary nor desirable.

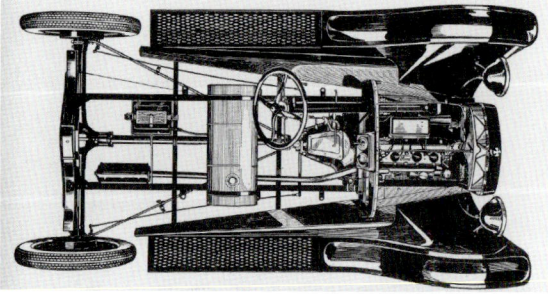

The Model T chassis showing its simple exhaust and silencer. No tail pipe after 1917. (Courtesy Ford Motor Co and MTFRGB)

Bodywork

Most Fords have steel panels on wooden frames. Some early cars had aluminum panels, and hoods (bonnets) were aluminum until 1915. The amount of wood decreased over the years, and the 'Improved' Ford cars from late 1925 only have wood in the roof and as trim 'tack strips.' Bodies were made in all styles, but the basic checks are similar: check for rust in steel panels, especially near the bottom of each one, and for rot in wood frames. Touring (open four-seater) bodies need careful checks for structural integrity below and in front of the rear doors; the whole rear body hangs from here. (1913 Touring cars may have visible steel reinforcement pieces).

The closed Centerdoor and Town Car bodies require careful inspection, as they are complex and expensive to restore.

Pre-1912 open cars had no front doors. US-built Touring cars had no left-side driver's door until late 1925 (because the handbrake would have made access difficult anyway). Most other cars had doors on both sides (including Canadian and UK vehicles, which were supplied to both LHD and RHD territories). Most doors and their mechanisms are very simple, but pre-1925 closed car doors are heavy and have straps or winders to lower the side windows. Check for hinge and lock wear.

Cowl (scuttle) and firewall (dashboard)

The shape and materials changed with the year. Check that it is correct for the date of build. The shaped metal cowl first appeared with the 1915 cars. Cars with starters, and all post-1921 vehicles, have an instrument panel. The panel should have an ammeter if a generator is fitted. Check that the wood is sound (pre-1924). Check the structural integrity on open cars by pulling on the screen. There are various designs of mounting brackets and straps.

Firewalls were wood until 1924. Touring Car screens were two-piece, carried in frames that bolted to the firewall. The only instruments were a speedometer on cars before mid-1914, and an ammeter on Fords with generators. (Courtesy Bob Richmon, Art Gergoudis and MTFCI)

Windshield (windscreen)

Open cars have separate frames which bolt onto the firewall. The details varied with the supplier, but all have two-piece screens. The top half can be adjusted or folded down. Early car screens have struts to the radiator mounts. Except for early cars, frames were painted black.

Closed car screens often have separate frames and can be opened in hot or misty weather.

Ask if 'safety' glass has been fitted. Check for cracks, scratches or discoloration. Check any sealing strips for perished rubber or signs of leaks.

Many Fords have an accessory wiper, with a hand-operated lever operated directly by the driver. This became standard on the 'Improved' 1926 models.

Fenders (wings) and running boards

First check whether the fenders (wings) are the correct shape for the claimed year of manufacture (see photo overleaf). There were detail changes to running boards' stamped patterns over the years. 'Improved' cars have a wider design.

Ford used good fairly thick materials so, although fenders may be bent, they are usually free of serious rust. Nevertheless, do check with your magnet. Look also

Early cars have flat-top fenders (wings) – there were detail changes during production to decorative ribs and the 'beak.' Curved fenders were fitted at the rear from 1915, and at the front from 1917. Running board stamped patterns changed over the years. 1926-7 'Improved' cars' fenders and running boards were wider.

for dings and dents, cracks resulting from vibration – and evidence of any earlier serious damage.

Paint

4 3 2 1

Don't be surprised if the vehicle is not black. The all-black policy only applied from 1914-1924 (1923 in the UK). Outside this time, Fords were available in other colors, and all coachbuilt and most commercial vehicles would be finished to customer choice. The quality of the paint finish on a Ford is, for many people, much less important than on more exotic cars. In fact, the rusty 'barn find' look is quite popular. However, if you buy a vehicle in that state, restoration is 'all or nothing.'

Trim

4 3 2 1

Open car seats were leather until mid-1913, when cheaper 'Leatherette' was introduced. Touring car front floors were covered by loose rubber mats; rear floors had cocoa mats – rubber from 1916. Closed cars had cloth (wool) seats and trim and carpets. Upholstery kits for most models (c1913 onwards) are available from US suppliers in materials and finishes close to the originals. Commercial vehicles had minimal trim or comforts.

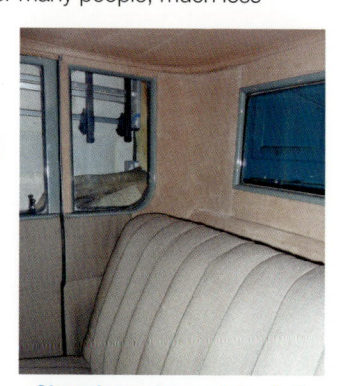

Closed cars have plain cloth headlinings. Seat and door coverings usually have a fine stripe.

Soft top

4 3 2 1

Frames have metal parts at the sides connecting to wooden 'bows' overhead. The wood can rot and the steel fittings can rust, and can be expensive to replace. An inspection should include erecting and folding the hood. Pre-1923 Touring cars require two people to do this; later tops can be managed by one person. Check all the outer fabric, including the fixings to the frame. Tops can shrink in cold weather, or if left folded. New fabric tops are available.

If there are side-screens with the car, check, fit and inspect these, too.

Pre-1923 Touring Car tops need two people to fold and erect.

Inside the cockpit 4 3 2 1

There is little to check that isn't covered in other parts of this chapter, but do assess the sitting position, and ease of entry and egress. Following the fashion for lower cars meant reducing legroom for the driver. Check that you can press the pedals. Check for modifications and accessories. Are they well installed and appropriate – and do you like them?

Speedometers were only fitted by the factory up to 1914, and were mostly supplied by Stewart. These, and their original drive cables and gears, are rare and valuable.

Shiny steering wheel and controls (ignition timing on the left; throttle on the right) on this 1912. (Courtesy Bob Richmon, Art Gergoudis and MTFCI)

Accessories 4 3 2 1

The Model T Ford fueled the growth of the car accessory industry, partly because of its huge sales volume, but also because Henry Ford refused to make his car more elaborate than absolutely necessary. Almost all surviving Model Ts have one or more accessories, most of them useful and desirable. Several have been mentioned in the sections above. Other common period or replica period accessories are mirrors, horns, spare wheel (or tire) carriers, luggage carriers (rear or running board), tool boxes, fuel can mounts, detachable wheels (or rims), wire wheels, speedometers, radiator thermometers, extra 'shock absorbers' (actually series coil springs), high-compression heads and, of course, auxiliary gearboxes and additional rear brakes. Many of these, notably Ruckstell and Warford Gearboxes, Rocky Mountain Brakes and 'Z' Heads are still made today.

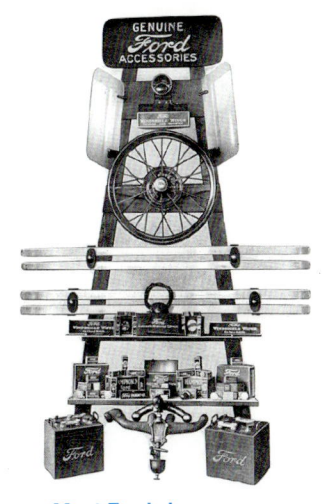

Most Fords have one or more accessories. (Courtesy Ford Motor Co and MTFRGB)

A complete tool kit for a 1912 Model T. (Courtesy Bob Richmon, Art Gergoudis and MTFCI)

39

Check to see what the vehicle has, and whether you approve. Note that, if a Warford-type auxiliary gearbox is fitted, it is possible to inadvertently select 'neutral,' which disconnects the main brake from the rear wheels. Auxiliary brakes are really essential with this type of gearbox unless, perhaps, it is an 'Improved' Ford with the larger more effective rear drums.

There are period (and replica) Ford tools for the Model T. You will need the hub-cap/sump wrench. The curved wrench (spanner) for the sparkplug/cylinder head and wheel nuts, and a rear hub remover are useful. Period wheel jacks are easy to find, too.

Cotter pins, wirelocking, nuts and bolts   [4] [3] [2] [1]

Ford made extensive use of cotter pins (split pins) – with good reason. A well-maintained car will have all these in place, so this check can be quite informative. Lock washers or 'stiff' nuts are acceptable, but not original, in some locations (typically around the block/oil pan joint). Check, especially, front and rear spring clamps and shackles, front axle 'perch' nuts, trackrod end bolts, Pitman arm nut (the arm on the lower end of the steering column), drag link bolts, steering spindle nuts, steering lower bracket nuts, rear radius rod nuts, brake clevis pins, radiator mounting nuts, and the front and center main bearing nuts. There *must* be wirelocking across the studs holding the cap at the rear of the front radius rods, and across the lower pair of bolts attaching the driveshaft to the transmission.

Most threads are what later became UNF, with some UNC. Fixings with these threads are common in the USA and still available elsewhere, so any Ford with odd mismatched bolts should be marked down. You may find Robertson screws with a square recess in Canadian-built bodies.

Safety modifications   [4] [3] [2] [1]

Unless you are looking for a static museum exhibit, we recommend that owners at least consider some simple changes and additions which will not only make driving easier and safer, but reduce the chances of upsetting other drivers. We should do all we can to delay the (inevitable?) day when 'authorities' restrict the use of old cars.

Lights are important. If you will drive at night or in poor visibility, you must be seen. As already mentioned, LED lights and bulbs are available to meet this need. Additional lights can clip on or even be attached by magnets, or they can fit inside old lights. You can just fit modern bulbs to original electric lights. As Ford only supplied an electric tail light on the driver's side, a second period or period-style lamp is recommended. Red reflectors can be added unobtrusively, and a magnetic reflective strip across the rear is a good idea, too.

Many Ford drivers still rely on hand

An electric tail light was fitted on the driver's side only. A second tail light, turn signals, and a brakelight are recommended for use today.

signals to indicate their intentions, but no modern driver is accustomed to watching for these. Much better to add discrete flashing indicators, especially to closed cars and trucks where the driver isn't visible – and may be sitting on the 'wrong' side. There are even 'wireless' turn-signal kits which clip onto any vehicle.

Most importantly, a Model T should have one or more brake lights. Modern drivers often encounter other users who don't use their turn signals, but they do *not* expect to follow a vehicle with no brakelight. It's easy to connect a switch to the brake pedal and fit a light at the rear.

The Ford was designed before safety entered anyone's mind. Experience has shown that accidents are rare, but cars have been hit from behind, and there have been front wheel or steering failures.

It isn't practical to fit seat belts to most Model Ts, but you can and should ensure that the windscreen (and side windows if relevant) are modern laminated safety glass. The original plate glass breaks into lethal shards.

Ford did not supply speedometers after 1914 (either because of cost, or reliability). You will not be driving fast, but knowing your speed – and how far you have traveled – is helpful.

Working original speedometer heads and drives are rare and very expensive, but a cycle speedometer, GPS or even a smartphone app are simple, accurate alternatives.

If you agree with the above, then include these features in your assessment. If modifications have been done, check whether they have been done well, and, if they aren't present, allow for the potential cost.

Starting   4 3 2 1

The vendor should be able to demonstrate starting and driving. If he or she cannot, then it is vital that you, or someone with you, has Model T driving experience to run and drive the vehicle.

Most Model Ts start quite easily. Even 'barn finds' can usually be made to run, with new fuel and a good battery.

You may be surprised to learn that it is fairly common to jack up one rear wheel and *release* the handbrake before starting a Model T if the weather and engine are cold. Releasing the handbrake engages the high gear clutch, thereby eliminating its drag, and adding rear wheel inertia to keep the engine turning. The other rear wheel must be 'chocked' securely.

The ignition must always be fully retarded (timing lever 'up') for starting. Advanced ignition will damage either the starter Bendix, or your hand or arm.

After turning on the fuel (tap below the tank), it's usually a good idea to turn a cold engine two turns, with the choke pulled and the ignition off. Then, with the choke 'off,' a little throttle (hand lever one-third down) and ignition turned to 'bat' (assuming it has a battery), the engine should fire, when spun with the starter or crank handle. When cranking, ensure your thumb and fingers are all on one side of the handle in case it kicks back.

As soon as the engine starts, advance the ignition (lever about halfway down) and adjust the throttle to achieve a good idle – not too fast or slow. After starting with a wheel raised, the handbrake can be applied, and the jack lowered, when the wheel has stopped. Let the engine run for a while and listen for knocks, exhaust or exhaust manifold 'blowing' or other worrying noises. If the seller will allow you, there is a useful check to be performed on coils and cylinders. With the engine running, remove the coil box lid. Set the engine at a fast idle, then hold down the lower points of coils two and three. This will prevent those cylinders firing. Don't touch the HT leads – everything else is safe. The engine should continue to run fairly smoothly on cylinders one and four. Then release coils two and three, and stop coils one and four, to check cylinders two and three. If the engine stops or runs badly during either check, one or both of the 'live' cylinders or coils has a problem. Note that, with the lid removed, you should see each coil firing – the points move.

Don't forget to check magneto function – the engine should run on 'bat' or 'mag.'

A warm engine can be started without jacking the rear wheel.

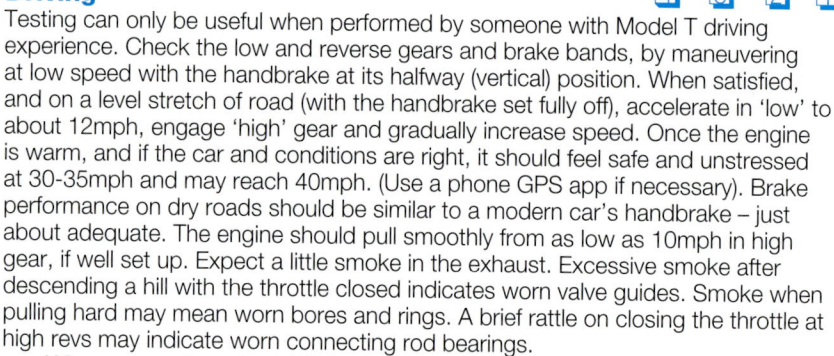

Driving [4] [3] [2] [1]

Testing can only be useful when performed by someone with Model T driving experience. Check the low and reverse gears and brake bands, by maneuvering at low speed with the handbrake at its halfway (vertical) position. When satisfied, and on a level stretch of road (with the handbrake set fully off), accelerate in 'low' to about 12mph, engage 'high' gear and gradually increase speed. Once the engine is warm, and if the car and conditions are right, it should feel safe and unstressed at 30-35mph and may reach 40mph. (Use a phone GPS app if necessary). Brake performance on dry roads should be similar to a modern car's handbrake – just about adequate. The engine should pull smoothly from as low as 10mph in high gear, if well set up. Expect a little smoke in the exhaust. Excessive smoke after descending a hill with the throttle closed indicates worn valve guides. Smoke when pulling hard may mean worn bores and rings. A brief rattle on closing the throttle at high revs may indicate worn connecting rod bearings.

When pressed, each pedal should be close to, but not touching, the floor or the ends of its slot. Earlier engagement will cause drag and band wear. Once engaged (pedal held down for low and reverse, pedals released for high), gears should not slip.

Steering should be direct and should self-center (going forward).

If an auxiliary gearbox is fitted, check its operation.

Roadworthiness test certificate [4] [3] [2] [1]

There are varied (or no) requirements for this in the USA – an important consideration if buying here. The UK MoT test is not required on pre-1960 vehicles. However, an independent test is worthwhile. Germany has its TUV or DEKRA test and France the Control Technique. Ask to see the latest certification and check its date. Failure information is as useful as a pass certificate.

Evaluation procedure

Add up the total points scored.

120 points = first class, possibly concours; 85 points = good/very good;
60 points = average; 35 points = poor.

A car scoring over 100 should be completely usable and require the minimum of repair, although continued maintenance and care will be required to keep it in condition. Cars scoring between 35 and 70 points will require a full restoration – the cost of which will be much the same, regardless of the points scored. Cars scoring between 70 and 100 points will require very careful assessment of the necessary repair/restoration costs, in order to decide a realistic purchase value.

10 Auctions
– sold! Another way to buy your dream

Auction pros & cons
Pros: Prices are often lower than those of dealers or private sellers and you might grab a real bargain on the day. Auctioneers have usually established clear title with the seller. At the venue, you can usually examine documentation relating to the vehicle.
Cons: You have to rely on a sketchy catalogue description of condition & history. The opportunity to inspect is limited and you cannot drive the car. Auction cars are often a little below par and may require some work. It's easy to overbid. There will usually be a buyer's premium to pay, in addition to the auction hammer price.

Which auction?
Auctions by established auctioneers are advertised in car magazines and on the auction houses' websites. A catalogue, or a simple printed list of the lots for auctions might only be available a day or two ahead, though often lots are listed and pictured on auctioneers' websites much earlier. Contact the auction company to ask if previous auction selling prices are available, as this is useful information (details of past sales are often available on websites).

Catalog, entry fee and payment details
When you purchase the catalog of the vehicles in the auction, it often acts as a ticket allowing two people to attend the viewing days and the auction. Catalog details tend to be comparatively brief, but will include information such as 'one owner since 1998, regularly used, full restoration history,' etc. It will also usually show a guide price to give you some idea of what to expect to pay and will tell you what is charged as a 'Buyer's premium.' The catalog will also contain details of acceptable forms of payment. At the fall of the hammer an immediate deposit is usually required, the balance payable within 24 hours. If the plan is to pay by cash there may be a cash limit. Some auctions will accept payment by debit card. Sometimes credit or charge cards are acceptable, but will often incur an extra charge. A bank draft or bank transfer will have to be arranged in advance with your own bank as well as with the auction house. No car will be released before *all* payments are cleared. If delays occur in payment transfers, then storage costs can accrue.

Buyer's premium
A buyer's premium will be added to the hammer price: *don't* forget this in your calculations. It is not usual for there to be a further state tax or local tax on the purchase price and/or on the buyer's premium. UK VAT may be payable if the seller is a business.

Viewing
In some instances, it's possible to view on the day, or days before, as well as in the hours prior to, the auction. There are auction officials available who are willing to help out by opening engine and luggage compartments and to allow you to inspect the interior. While the officials may start the engine for you, a test drive is out of the question. Crawling under and around the car as much as you want is permitted, but you can't suggest that the car you are interested in be jacked up, or attempt to do the job yourself. You can also ask to see any documentation available.

Bidding

Before you take part in the auction, *decide your maximum bid – and stick to it!*

It may take a while for the auctioneer to reach the lot you are interested in, so use that time to observe how other bidders behave. When it's the turn of your car, attract the auctioneer's attention and make an early bid. The auctioneer will then look to you for a reaction every time another bid is made, usually the bids will be in fixed increments until the bidding slows, when smaller increments will often be accepted before the hammer falls. If you want to withdraw from the bidding, make sure the auctioneer understands your intentions – a vigorous shake of the head when he or she looks to you for the next bid should do the trick!

Assuming that you are the successful bidder, the auctioneer will note your card or paddle number, and from that moment on you will be responsible for the vehicle.

If the car is unsold, either because it failed to reach the reserve or because there was little interest, it may be possible to negotiate with the owner, via the auctioneers, after the sale is over.

Successful bid

There are two more items to think about. How to get the car home, and insurance. You probably won't want to drive the car. Your own or a hired trailer is one way, another is to have the vehicle shipped using the facilities of a local company. The auction house will also have details of companies specializing in the transfer of cars.

Insurance for immediate cover can usually be purchased on site, but it may be more cost-effective to make arrangements with your own insurance company in advance, and then call to confirm the full details.

eBay & other online auctions?

eBay & other online auctions could land you a car at a bargain price, though you'd be foolhardy to bid without examining the car first, something most vendors encourage. A useful feature of eBay is that the geographical location of the car is shown, so you can narrow your choices to those within a realistic radius of home. Be prepared to be outbid in the last few moments of the auction. Remember that your bid is binding and it will be very, very difficult to get restitution in the case of a crooked vendor fleecing you – *caveat emptor!*

Be aware that some cars offered for sale in online auctions are 'ghost' cars. *Don't* part with *any* cash without being sure that the vehicle does actually exist and is as described (usually pre-bidding inspection is possible).

Auctioneers

Barrett-Jackson barrett-jackson.com, Bonhams bonhams.com,
British Car Auctions BCA) bca-europe.com, or british-car-auctions.co.uk,
Cheffins cheffins.co.uk, Christies christies.com, Coys coys.co.uk,
eBay eBay.com, H&H handh.co.uk, RM rmauctions.com, Shannons shannons.com,
Silver silverauctions.com, Herefordshire Vintage Auctions hvauctions.com,
DVCA dvca.co.uk, Richard Edmonds richardedmondsauctions.com.

Also look at local auctioneers, including agricultural. Magazines such as *The Automobile* often include auction previews.

11 Paperwork
– correct documentation is essential!

The paper trail
Veteran, vintage and collectors' cars usually come with a large portfolio of paperwork accumulated and passed on by a succession of proud owners. This documentation represents the real history of the car and from it can be deduced the level of care the car has received, how much it's been used, which specialists have worked on it and the dates of major repairs and restorations. All of this information will be priceless to you as the new owner, so be very wary of a car with little paperwork to support its claimed history – unless it is a genuine 'barn find.'

Registration documents
All countries/states have some form of registration for private vehicles, whether it's the American Title ('pink slip') system or the British 'log book' system.

It is essential to check that the registration document is genuine, that it relates to the car in question, and that all the vehicle's details are correctly recorded, including chassis and engine numbers (if these are shown). If you are buying from the previous owner, his or her name and address will be recorded in the document: this will not be the case if you are buying from a dealer.

In the UK, the current (Euro-aligned) registration document is named 'V5C,' and is printed in colored sections of red, blue, green and yellow. The blue section relates to the car specification, the green section has details of the owner and another green section is sent to the DVLA in the UK when the car is sold. A small section in yellow deals with selling the car within the motor trade. A further blue section is used when a vehicle is exported.

In the UK, the DVLA will provide available details of earlier keepers of the vehicle upon payment of a fee, but usually only those after about 1980.

It may be wise to check for liens (debts) against the Title or V5C.

If the car has a foreign registration, there may be expensive and time-consuming formalities to complete. If importing a car, it is vital to have the 'Title' or other registration documentation from the exporting country. A car imported into the UK will have to go through the NOVA (Notice Of Vehicle Arrival) process.

Roadworthiness certificate
Most country/state administrations require that vehicles are regularly tested to prove that they are safe to use on the public highway and do not produce excessive emissions. In the USA the requirement varies, but most states insist on an emissions test every two years as a minimum, while the police are charged with pulling over unsafe-looking vehicles.

If the car has been entered in tours in the USA organized by the MTFCA or MTFCI, the owner should have completed and submitted roadworthiness inspection forms. Ask if these are available.

In the UK, pre-1960 cars (ie all Model Ts) are now exempt from the annual 'MoT' inspection (a roadworthiness test). However, tests *were* required prior to 2012, and old certificates provide a useful independent record of that car's history. Ask the seller if previous certificates are available.

Road license
The administration of every country/state requires some form of 'road license.' How it is displayed varies enormously from country to country and state to state.

Whatever the form of the 'road license,' it must relate to the vehicle carrying it and must be present and valid if the car is to be driven on the public highway legally. The value of the license will depend on the length of time it will continue to be valid.

In the UK, if a car is untaxed because it is not being used for a period of time, the owner has to inform the licensing authorities (via the SORN system), otherwise the vehicle's date-related registration number will be lost and there will be a painful amount of paperwork to get it re-registered. In the UK, vehicles built before the end of 1973 (all Model Ts) are licensed free of charge, but there is still an annual renewal with DVLA.

Certificates of authenticity
For many makes of collectable car, it is possible to get a certificate declaring the age and authenticity (based on engine and chassis numbers and key dating features) of a particular vehicle. These are sometimes called 'Heritage Certificates,' and if the car comes with one of these it is a definite bonus. If you want to obtain one, the relevant owners' club is the best starting point.

Pre-1919 Fords are eligible for Veteran Car Club events in the UK once the owner has a VCC dating document.

If the car has been used in European classic car rallies it may have a FIVA (Federation Internationale des Vehicules Anciens) certificate. The so-called 'FIVA Passport,' or 'FIVA Vehicle Identity Card,' enables organizers and participants to recognise whether or not a particular vehicle is suitable for individual events. If you want to obtain such a certificate go to www.fbhvc.co.uk or www.fiva.org There will be similar organizations in other countries, too.

If the car has claims to be Concours standard, it may have been entered in a formal competition, such as those organized by the MTFCI, and have been given a formal documented assessment indicating not only the standard of each part of the car, but also whether it is 'correct.'

Valuation certificate
Hopefully, the vendor will have a recent valuation certificate, or letter signed by a recognized expert stating how much he or she believes the particular car to be worth (such documents, together with photos, are usually needed to get 'agreed value' insurance). Generally such documents should act only as confirmation of your own assessment of the car rather than a guarantee of value as the expert may not have seen the car in the flesh. The easiest way to find out how to obtain a formal valuation is to contact the owners' club. Note that a valuation for insurance is not the same as market value.

Service history
Most Model Ts will have been serviced at home by enthusiastic (and hopefully capable) owners for a good number of years. Nevertheless, try to obtain as much service history and other paperwork pertaining to the car as you can. Naturally, specialist garage receipts score most points in the value stakes. However, anything helps in the great authenticity game. A bill of sale, handbook, parts invoices and repair bills, photographs add to the story and the character of the car. Even a

brochure correct to the year of the car's manufacture is a useful document and something that you could well have to search hard to locate in future years. If the seller claims that the car has been restored, then expect receipts and other evidence from a specialist restorer or parts supplier.

If the seller claims to have carried out regular servicing, ask what work was completed, when, and seek some evidence of it being carried out. Your assessment of the car's overall condition should tell you whether the seller's claims are genuine.

Restoration photographs
If the seller tells you that the car has been restored, then expect to be shown a series of photographs taken while the restoration was under way. Pictures taken at various stages, and from various angles, should help you gauge the thoroughness of the work. Old photos may provide valuable evidence of registration number. If you buy the car, ask if you can have all the photographs as they form an important part of the vehicle's history. It's surprising how many sellers are happy to part with their car and accept your cash, but want to hang on to their photographs! In the latter event, you may be able to persuade the vendor to get a set of copies made.

The sporty Model T – not ideal for this Scottish rain: a 1911 Torpedo.

www.velocebooks.com / www.veloce.co.uk
Details of all current books • New book news • Special offers • Gift vouchers • Forum

47

12 What's it worth?
– let your head rule your heart

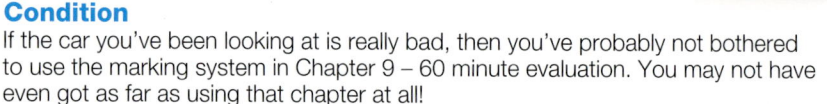

Condition
If the car you've been looking at is really bad, then you've probably not bothered to use the marking system in Chapter 9 – 60 minute evaluation. You may not have even got as far as using that chapter at all!

If you did use the marking system in Chapter 9, you'll know whether the car is in Excellent (maybe Concours), Good, Average or Poor condition, or somewhere in-between these categories.

Many classic/collector car magazines run a regular price guide. If you haven't bought the latest editions, do so now, and compare their suggested values for the model you are thinking of buying: also look at the auction prices they're reporting. Values of good examples of most classic cars have risen since savings interest rates have been very low, but some models will always be more sought-after than others. Trends can change, too. The values published in the magazines tend to vary from one magazine to another, as do their scales of condition, so read carefully the guidance notes they provide. Bear in mind that a car that is truly a recent show winner could be worth more than the highest scale published. Assuming that the car you have in mind is not in show/concours condition, then relate the level of condition that you judge the car to be in with the appropriate guide price. How does the figure compare with the asking price? Before you start haggling with the seller, consider what effect any variation from standard specification might have on the car's value.

If you are buying from a dealer, remember there will be a dealer's premium within the price. Ask the dealer if he owns the vehicle, or if he is selling on commission.

Desirable options/extras
Almost all Model Ts have one or more 'extras' – even just a spare tire carrier or fuel can clamp, and most of these are desirable to some extent. Those that significantly

Ford did not supply a speedometer from mid-1914, but accessories were available. This is an original 1912 instrument.
(Courtesy Bob Richmon, Art Gergoudis and MTFCI)

affect the vehicle's value include an auxiliary gearbox (such as the Ruckstell or Warford), auxiliary brakes (eg Rocky Mountain), an original period speedometer and, much rarer, exotic OHV or even OHC cylinder heads. Never decline spare parts, unless the price is very unreasonable.

Undesirable features
Any Model T with any sort of modern – or other non-standard – engine, transmission or rear axle is best avoided, unless you have original parts and the ability to restore it. Many Model Ts suffered at the hands of 'Hot Rodders.' This book is not for them.

'Bitsa' cars – vehicles which are an obvious mix of parts from different years must be considered very carefully. It used to be fashionable to fit a brass radiator and early hood (bonnet) to later Model Ts, and examples still come on the market. You will be wise to budget for putting things right. Avoid buying a vehicle which has suffered 'butchering' which cannot be reversed.

For most people, modern paint colors (especially metallic) and any application of chromium plating are not appropriate for a Model T.

Striking a deal
Negotiate on the basis of your condition assessment, the history/ownership record, mileage, and fault rectification cost. Also take into account the car's specification. Be realistic about the value, but don't be completely intractable: a small compromise on the part of the vendor or buyer will often facilitate a deal at little real cost. If the price seems very low, you need to understand why.

Speedometers were driven by gears from the front right wheel.
(Courtesy Bob Richmon, Art Gergoudis and the MTFCI)

13 Do you really want to restore?
– it'll take longer and cost more than you think

The real questions are, how much restoration are you willing to take on, and who is going to do it? Some people are quite happy to do major mechanical work, but not bodywork, trim, or, more often, electrical work. The usual advice – 'buy the best you can afford' – may not always apply here, because a Model T is one of the easiest old vehicles to restore if you have the will. It can be difficult judging which is the best, and whether it is as good as it may seem, but this book should help you to minimize later disappointment.

A conservative estimate is that 50,000 Model Ts survive (some people claim double that number – it depends on what you count as a vehicle).

Fords can still be found in rough condition in barns. You might think that being stored away for 60 years or more means that a car will be basically good, but this is not always the case. Most Model Ts were bought to be used, and they were worked until they wore out. However, if you find an example which is *complete* – nothing removed or partly disassembled – it may well be worth taking on. Beware of buying any old car in pieces, and beware if the engine is 'unsealed' – cylinder head, hog's head or crankcase removed. Water and rodent or insect life are not good for the internal parts.

The year of the vehicle matters, too. An early brass radiator car will require a lot of time, effort and money to find or replicate missing parts, but you may eventually have a very rare, very old and valuable car with lots of polished brass. If your desire is just to join other owners driving Model Ts, on a tour or just to buy an ice cream, as soon as possible, find a later example for which parts – new and used – are readily available and not expensive.

You may be surprised to have read here that the Ford is easy to restore, but it was designed to be assembled as easily and quickly as possible, and millions were kept going by 'shade tree' mechanics. Everything is bolted or screwed together (except for the riveted chassis frame). A Model T can be taken apart in less than a day. There is no spot-welded bodyshell (except 1926-7 cars which have a few such welds), no hydraulic system, only the simplest electrical system, and no computers. The threads are almost all what later became UNF (with a few UNC), and you need only two or three simple special tools. Furthermore, Henry Ford used good materials throughout – his parts have stood the test of time, and steel panels are thicker than usual. Other than in speedometers and drives, there is no 'Mazak' alloy to crumble away.

Mechanically sound, but not a concours winner. Sue and James Colman have enjoyed years of touring in their 'oily rag' black-radiator Model T Touring Car.

If the engine is completely worn out, you will have to use specialists to replace white metal main and connecting rod bearings. Competent white-metallers are becoming rarer. You may also need specialists to regrind the crank, rebore cylinders, replace valve seats and perhaps repair cracks in the block or head. A transmission overhaul may require access to an hydraulic press and reamers. Wooden wheel spoke replacement also requires a press, but this can be home-made. Trembler coils should be set up using the original Ford test tool, or a modern equivalent.

Everything else is within the scope of many owners. Almost all mechanical parts are readily available at affordable prices. New fenders (wings), running boards and other panels are available for most years, as are complete trim kits for most factory body styles. Help in the form of books, videos, on-line advice and forums and assistance from other enthusiasts is abundant. See Chapter 16.

Engines left without cylinder heads and crankcases corrode inside. Probably salvageable, but costly.

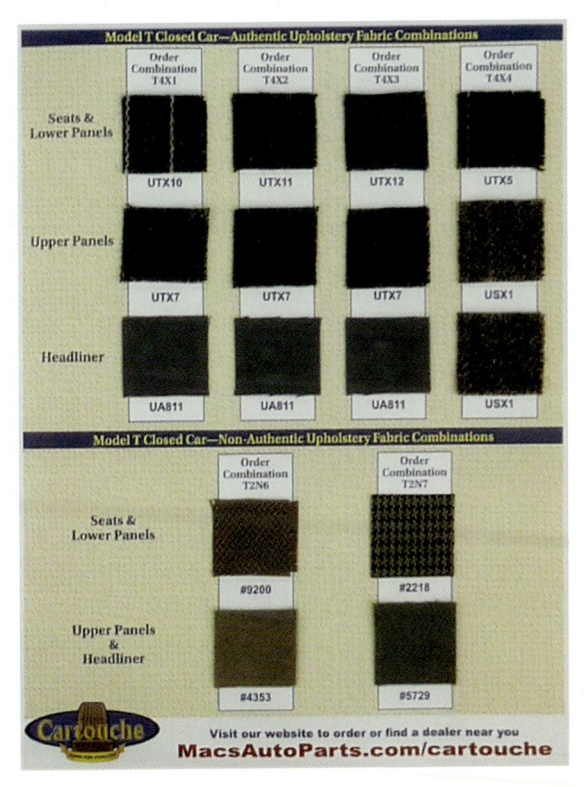

Fabric and carpet samples in original colors and styles in a MACS 'Cartouch' brochure.

51

14 Paint problems
– bad complexion, including dimples, pimples and bubbles

The paint finish can dominate one's first impression of a classic car. However, the design and character of the car are such that, for many people, paint somehow matters less on a Model T Ford. A few owners actually prefer the 'oily rag' look (ie the bodywork has been restored just by wiping with an oily rag). If you buy a car in this state, you either leave it alone or restore everything.

• Paint faults generally occur due to lack of protection/maintenance, or to poor preparation prior to a respray or touch-up. However, people have been restoring Model Ts for more than 50 years, so many cars' paint problems, such as fading, are just those of age.

• Blistering is almost always caused by corrosion of the metal beneath the paint and things are usually worse than they seem.

• Orange peel, cracking, crazing, micro blistering and peeling usually result from poor preparation for, or application of, primer and paint. Orange peel may be remedied by abrasives and polish; other faults generally require rub-down or strip and respray. Model T panels are usually removed for respraying.

• The all-black period did not begin until 1914, but original Ford dark colors, such as the blue and green, used before this time darken with age and appear to be black

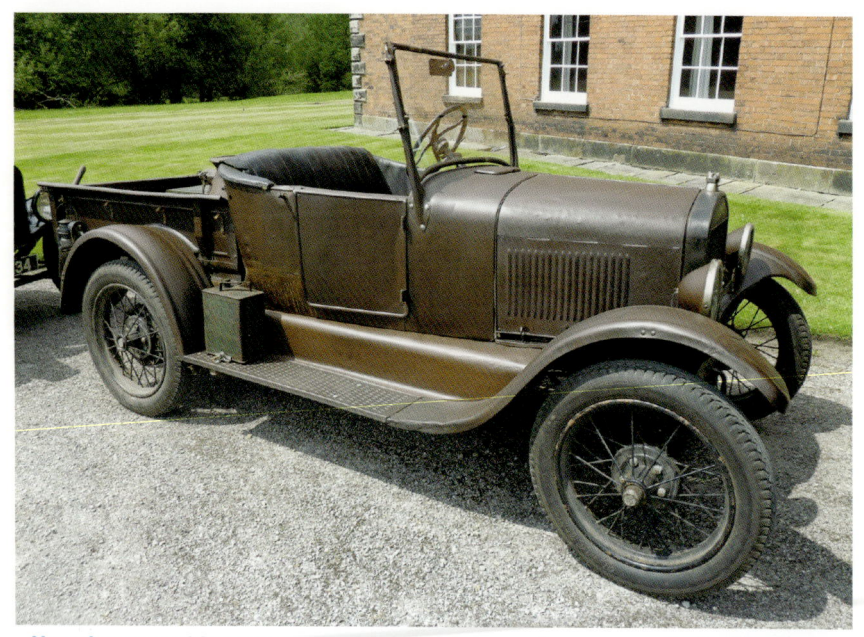

No paint, no problem: this car with a pickup rear end was rescued after 60 years in the desert. It has a few bullet holes, but its mechanical parts have been restored, and now it is used and enjoyed.

15 Problems due to lack of use

– just like their owners, Model Ts need exercise!

Cars, like humans, are at their most efficient if they exercise regularly. A run of at least ten miles, once a week, is recommended for classics. Just starting an engine for a few minutes is bad practice.

Seized components
- Pistons can seize in the bores due to corrosion, especially if water has entered the engine
- Transmission bushes can seize, if water has entered the engine
- Rear axle gears and bearings will suffer, if water enters the housings
- The commutator or timer can suffer from disuse
- Steering spindles can become very stiff, if left unlubricated
- Wheel bearings can seize, if water displaces the grease
- Parking brakes (handbrakes) can seize, if the linkages and cams rust

Fluids
- Old, acidic oil can corrode bearings
- Uninhibited coolant can corrode internal waterways. Lack of antifreeze can cause core plugs to be pushed out and even cracks in the block or head. Silt settling and solidifying can cause subsequent overheating
- Fuel is an increasing problem. Modern fuels containing ethanol degrade very quickly – a matter of weeks. They also soften old deposits, absorb water and either attack or block up tanks, pipes and carburettors. Additives can delay some of these effects and should be used if a Ford is stored for any significant period and fuel is not drained

Tire (tyre) problems
- Tires that have had the weight of the car on them in a single position for some time will develop flat spots, resulting in some (usually temporary) vibration. The tire walls may have cracks or (blister-type) bulges, meaning new tires are needed. Barn-find Fords may even have tires made before WWII. Note that all Model Ts have inner tubes

Springs
- The front and rear springs benefit from grease between their leaves. Otherwise, corrosion forms, which makes the springs very stiff, and results in wear when driven

Fabric, rubber and plastic
- Tops (hoods) of open cars may shrink, if left folded. Many can be reclaimed by gradually applying tension in warm sun, but some will need an extra strip of material added
- There are just three short straight water hoses. These are cheap and easy to replace
- Rubber tubing in the fuel system added by earlier owners could well be very old, and is likely to be adversely affected by modern fuel containing ethanol. Replacement by metal pipes is *strongly* recommended
- Fan belts can harden or rot

Electrics
• The battery will be of little use if it has not been charged for many months
• Earthing/grounding problems are common, when the connections have corroded
• Sparkplug electrodes will often have corroded in an unused engine
• Wiring insulation can harden and fail
• The contacts in the coil box are often corroded or dirty. Damp coil box wood may cause 'tracking' of current away from the sparkplugs
• Trembler coil points will not perform well if they have corroded, and most original paper/foil capacitors in the coils are now in need of replacement

Wood
• Look for worm or rot in wheels spokes and felloes, and in body frames

Rotting exhaust system
• Exhaust gas contains a high water content, so exhaust systems corrode very quickly from the inside, when the car is not used

1915 English coachbuilt butcher's van in its original livery.

www.velocebooks.com / www.veloce.co.uk
Details of all current books • New book news • Special offers • Gift vouchers • Forum

16 The Community
– key people, organizations and companies in the Model T world

Clubs
North America
Model T Ford Club of America (MTFCA)
PO BOX 996, 309 N 8th Street, Richmond IN 47375-0996. Tel: 765 855-5248
Web: mtfca.com
 The MTFCA has 'chapters' in most US states and in other countries including Canada and Holland. It has a well-used and searchable technical forum: mtfca.com/discus/

Model T Ford Club International (MTFCI)
PO Box 355, Hudson, NC 28638-0355. Tel: 828 728-5758 Web: modelt.org
 The MTFCI has 'chapters' in most US states and in other countries in North and South America, Europe and Australia.

Europe
Model T Ford Register of Great Britain
195 Bradford Rd, Riddlesden, Keighley BD20 5JR Web: modeltregister.co.uk
Facebook: facebook.com/MTFRGB/
The UK club, founded in 1961, with 500 members.

Ford Model T en France
Web: ford-t.jimdo.com

The Irish Model T Ford Club
Web: irishmodeltclub.ie

Model T Club of Denmark
Web: ford-t.dk

Rest of the World
Model T Ford Club of Australia
Web: modeltfordclubaustralia.org.au

Model T Ford Club of Victoria (Australia)
The Model T Ford Club of Victoria Inc, PO Box 383, Chadstone Centre VIC 3148
Web: mtfcv.com

Model T Ford Club of Australia (NSW)
134 Queens Road Fivedock NSW – PO Box 2658 North Parramatta NSW 1750
Web: modeltfordclubnsw.org.au

Model T Owners Queensland
PO Box 50, Forest Hill, Queensland, 4342, Australia
Web: mtoq12.wixsite.com/mtoq

Veteran Car Club of WA – Model T-Ford Section
Veteran Car Club of WA [Inc]. PO Box 79, Bentley, WA 6982
Web: veterancarclubofwa.asn.au/branches-sections/model-t-ford

Model T Ford Club of New Zealand (Inc)
The Treasurer. PO Box 379, Te Kuiti 3910
Web: modeltford.co.nz/motor-pioneers/

Club del Ford T de Argentina
c/o Daniel Bollo. San Luis 2728, 5010 Cordoba, Argentina. Web: fordt.org.ar

No-one in sight, but this varied selection of Model Ts is on a UK tour with MTFRGB. (Courtesy MTFRGB)

Parts and Service Suppliers
USA
Lang's Lang's Old Car Parts, 74 Maple Street, Baldwinville MA, 01436
Tel: 1-800 872 7871 or 978 939 5500 Web: modeltford.com
Snyder's 12925 Woodworth Rd, New Springfield, Ohio 44443
Tel: 330 549 5313 Web: snydersantiqueauto.com
Chaffin's Chaffin's Garage, Inc, 1931 South Main St. Corona California 92882
Tel: 951 735 4791 Web: chaffinsgarage.com
Macs 6150 Donner Road, Lockport NY 14094
Tel: 716 210 1340 Web: macsautoparts.com
Bob's Antique Auto Parts 7826 Forest Hills Road, Loves Park, Illinois 61111
Tel: 815 633 7244 Web: bobsantiqueautoparts.com
Texas T Parts by Birdhaven Vintage Auto Supply, 3515 West 88th Street North, Colfax, IA 50054
Tel: 515 674 3949 Web: texastparts.com/mm5/merchant.mvc
Model T Haven 2031 Nebraska Rd, Iola, KS 66749
Tel: 620 365 6709 Web: modelthaven.com
Rootlieb 815 S Soderquist, Tulrock, CA 95380 (Sheet metal parts)
Tel: 209 632 2203 Web: rootlieb.com/home.html
Fun Projects, Inc 902 S Randall Rd, Suite C281, St Charles, IL 60174
Tel: 630 584 1471 Web: funprojects.com/contact.aspx

UK
Model T Ford Register of Great Britain (Members only)
Email: spares@modelregister.co.uk
Tel: (44) 1433 670420 Web: modelregister.co.uk/club-spares/spares-info.html
Tuckett Brothers Marstonfields, North Marston, Bucks, MK18 3PG
Tel: (44) 1296 670500 Web: modeltford.co.uk
T Service Ltd Unit 1b, Staplehurst Business Centre, Weston On The Green, Oxfordshire, OX25 3QU
Tel: (44) 1869 351006 Web: tservice.co.uk

Tudor Wheels St Jacques Cottage, Old Romsey Road, Cadnam, Southampton
SO40 2NP
Tel: (44) 7801 069261 Web: tudorwheels.co.uk

Australia
Henry's 129 Ballanee Road, Ballan, Victoria, Australia, 3342
Tel: (61) 03 5368 1088 Web: henryspares.com.au

Useful books
Ford Service Manual (Factory workshop manual for all Model Ts, available as a reprint)
Model T Ford – The Car That Changed The World (Full history and descriptions of all US-built cars. Bruce W McCalley. Incorporates material from his earlier *Model T Ford Encyclopedia*)
The Model T Ford Owner (Reprint of period DIY maintenance articles. Murray Fahnestock)
Repairing and Restoring the Model T Ford (Six books covering the mechanical systems of the Model T. Published by MTFCA)
The English Model T Ford Volume 1 (Full history of UK factory cars and trucks. Lilleker, Riley, Tuckett)
The English Model T Ford Volume 2 (Full history of UK coachbuilt cars and trucks, conversions, accessories and operation. Barker, Lilleker, Tuckett)
The Model T Ford Car (Unofficial owners' manual, published 1915-1918 USA. Pagé)
Ford Model T Instruction Books and Manuals (Original and reprinted owners' handbooks)
Ford Model T Parts Lists (Original and reprinted parts lists for most model years are useful for illustrations and for part numbers. Modern suppliers still use original part numbers)
The Book of the Ford* (Nicholson. Ten editions of this unofficial manual published in the UK, 1915-1927)
Tin Lizzie* (A delightful history and description. Philip Van Doren Stern, 1955)
Tin Lizzie (A great children's story covering the long life of a Model T. Peter Spier)
*Available used only.

Catalogues produced by most of the US parts suppliers are well-illustrated and useful. Most can be found online.
 There are also numerous books about, and biographies of, Henry Ford and his company

The Henry Ford Museum
20900 Oakwood Boulevard, Dearborn, MI 48124-5029
Call center: 313-982-6001 or 800-835-5237 Web: thehenryford.org
 Visit Greenfield Village, The Henry Ford Museum or take a Rouge factory tour. There is also an archive where you can access original documents and drawings.

17 Vital statistics
– essential data at your fingertips

Production history – engine numbers and prices

Year	USA engines Last number	Built	Canada engines Last number	Built	Touring Car price USA in $	UK in £
1908	309	309				
1909	14151	13842			850	245
1910	34899	20748			950	200
1911	88900	54001			780	190
1912	183563	94663			690	170
1913	408347	224784	C 12000	12000	600	150
1914	656063	247716	C 24000	12000	550	135
1915	1028313	372250	C 55000	31000	490	135
1916	1614516	586203	C 75000	20000	440	135
1917	2449179	834663	C 144000	69000	360	–
1918	2831426	382247	C 186000	42000	450	–
1919	3659971	828545	C 231000	45000	525	250
1920	4698419	1038448	C 281000	50000	675	275
1921	5638071	939652	C 319000	38000	510	220
1922	6953071	1315000	C 375000	56000	443	195
1923	9008371	2055300	C 456000	81000	380	148
1924	10994033	1985662	C 537000	81000	375	125
1925	12990076	1996043	C 616000	89000	375	125
1926	14619254	1629178	C 717000	101000	380	125
1927	15007032	387778	C 787000	70000	380	125

• The table above has been compiled from data in *Model T Ford – The Car That Changed The World* by Bruce McCalley and *The English Model T Ford – A Century of the Model T in Britain* by Riley, Lilleker and Tuckett. 'Last number' refers to the last engine built in a *calendar* year
• The 'built' column approximates to vehicle production as engines were usually used soon after manufacture. Model T engine production continued after US vehicle production ended in May 1927, only ceasing in 1941 when a further 170,000 engines had been produced
• The USA figures include engines used in the 301,000 Model Ts built at Trafford Park in the UK and 10,000 in Cork, Ireland
• Canadian figures are approximate. Canada also built about 15,000 Model Ts from 1909-1912
• Canada supplied not only its own market, but also British Empire countries including Australia, New Zealand and South Africa

General data

	Car	Ton truck
Length	12ft (3.66m)[1]	16ft (4.9m)[2]
Width	66in (1.68m)	68in (1.73m)[2]
Track	56in (1.42m)	56in (1.42m)
Wheelbase	100in (2.54m)	124in (3.15m)
Axle ratio	3.64:1	5.17:1 or 7.25:1
Max speed	42mph	33mph or 24mph
Weight	1600lb (725kg)[1]	2200lb (998kg)[2]
Fuel capacity	10 gal (US), 8.3gal (Imp), 38 liters[1]	
Oil capacity	1 gal (US), 0.83gal (Imp), 3.8 liters	
Bore	3.75in (95mm)	
Stroke	4.0in (102mm)	
Capacity	177cu in (2896cc)	
Max power	20bhp @ 1600rpm	
Max torque	85lbft @ 1100rpm	
Gear ratios Low	2.75:1	
High	1:1	
Reverse	4:1	

Notes:
1. Typical for Touring Car
2. Typical; depends on body

Paint colors – a summary

1909	Red, green, gray
1910	Dark green
1911-13	Dark blue (mid-green UK 1913)
1913-25	Black
1926-27	Black, Channel Green, Windsor Maroon, Highland Green, Royal Maroon, Fawn Gray, Gunmetal Blue, Phoenix Brown, Commercial Green, Moleskin, Drake Green.

Manchester cars were available in 'Empire Grey' from 1924, plus 'Orriford Lake' (dark red) or Cobalt Blue from 1925 and Carmine Lake, Moleskin Grey and Coach Green for 1926.

The Essential Buyer's Guide™ series ...

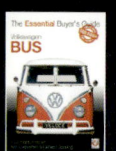

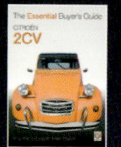

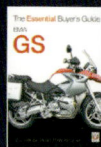

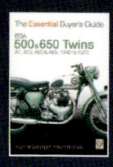

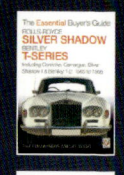

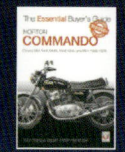

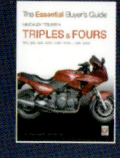

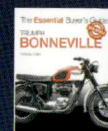

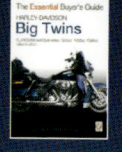

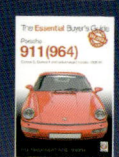

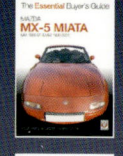

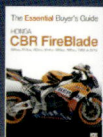

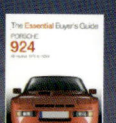

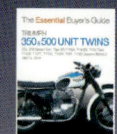

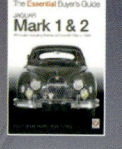

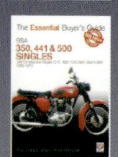

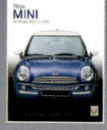

... don't buy a vehicle until you've read one of these!

For more details visit www.veloce.co.uk
or email info@veloce.co.uk

Also from Veloce Publishing –

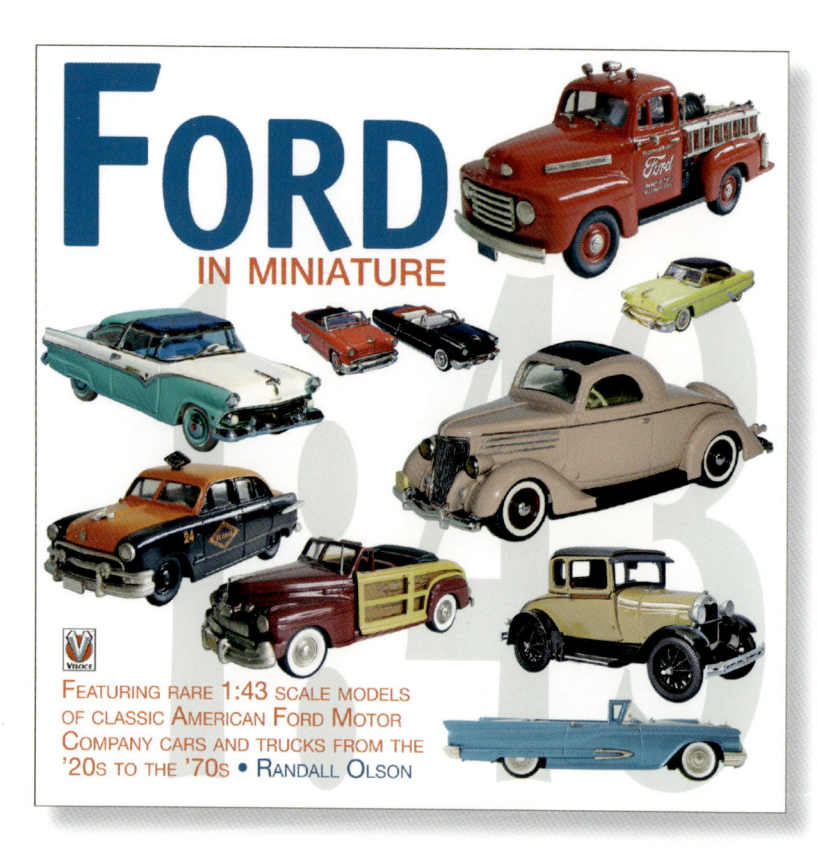

FORD IN MINIATURE

FEATURING RARE 1:43 SCALE MODELS OF CLASSIC AMERICAN FORD MOTOR COMPANY CARS AND TRUCKS FROM THE '20s TO THE '70s • RANDALL OLSON

This colourful eBook features some of the most beautiful and rare scale models of American Ford (including Edsel, Lincoln, and Mercury) cars and trucks from the classic 1930-69 period.

eBook ISBN: 978-1-845846-82-4
• Fixed layout • 128 pages • 440 colour pictures

For more info on Veloce titles, visit our website at www.veloce.co.uk
• email: info@veloce.co.uk • Tel: +44(0)1305 260068

Choosing the right oils & greases for your vintage, antique, classic or collector car

Which Oil?

Richard Michell

This book gives classic/collector car owners the information necessary to make an appropriate and safe choice of lubricants from the vast and sometimes overwhelming range available today.

ISBN: 978-1-845843-65-6
Paperback • 19.5x13.9cm • 128 pages
• 36 b&w pictures and line drawings

For more info on Veloce titles, visit our website at www.veloce.co.uk
• email: info@veloce.co.uk • Tel: +44(0)1305 260068

Index

Accessories 10, 15, 20, 21, 30, 39, 48
Auctions 43
Axle, front 22, 26
Axle, rear 22, 24, 27, 36, 59

Bands 10, 12, 13, 30, 31, 42
Bodywork 9, 10, 14, 16, 20, 22, 23, 28, 36, 50, 52, 59
Books 13, 24, 57
Brakes 6, 8, 11-13, 15, 22, 27, 28, 30, 39, 42, 53

Canada 9, 55, 58
Carburettor 10, 12, 35
Centerdoor 14, 37
Chassis (frame) 6, 21, 28, 31, 35, 36
Clubs 10, 46, 55, 56
Coachbuilt Fords 15, 16, 23, 38
Coil box 32, 33, 54
Coils (trembler) 8, 10, 13, 21, 32, 41, 42, 54
Commutator (timer) 8, 10, 13, 21, 32, 53
Controls 6, 11, 24, 39
Conversions 3, 15, 16, 17, 25, 29, 30, 34
Cotter pins (split pins) 13, 40
Coupe 7, 14, 15
Crankcase (oil pan) 30, 31
Cylinder head 10, 15, 17, 29

Depot Hack 7, 9, 17
Dimensions 6, 59,
Driving 6, 8, 11, 13, 20, 22, 40, 42

Early cars 9, 24, 27, 28, 37, 38
Electrical system 21, 33, 34, 40, 54
Engine 10, 11, 15, 24, 28-32, 41, 42, 51, 58, 59
Engine number 18, 21, 28, 58
Engine oil 7, 13, 30, 33, 59
Exhaust 10, 36, 41, 54

Fenders (wings) 10, 35-38
Firewall 21, 32, 37

Fordor 14, 35
Fuel consumption 7
Fuel tank 12

Gearbox (transmission) – stock 6, 30, 31, 42
Generator 9, 10, 21, 29, 33, 34, 37

Hog's head 29-31, 34
Hood (bonnet) 17, 36, 49
Hood (top) 6-8, 10, 12, 22, 38, 53

Ignition system 8, 13, 21, 32, 33, 39, 41
Inspection 18, 19, 45
Investment 8

Landaulette 6, 7, 14
LHD 10, 11, 17, 30, 37
Lights 13, 21, 34, 40, 41

Magneto 21, 32-34, 42
Maintenance 7, 8, 13, 40, 57
Manchester (Trafford Park) 3, 15, 26, 59
Model T Ford Club of America (MTFCA) 45, 55
Model T Ford Club International (MTFCI) 45, 46, 55
Model T Ford Register of Great Britain 3, 10, 55, 56
Model years 3, 21, 24, 57

OHV, OHC 15, 17, 20, 49

Paint 21, 38, 49, 52, 59,
Paperwork 45-47
Parts cost 3, 7, 9, 10, 51, 57
Parts suppliers 7, 10, 56
Production 9, 21, 24, 58

Radiator 9, 10, 14, 21, 22, 28, 50
Restoration 9, 21, 22, 37, 47, 50, 52, 57
RHD 10, 11, 17, 37
Roadworthiness checks 18, 21, 42, 45

Rocky Mountain brakes 8, 12, 17, 27, 39, 49,
Ruckstell gearbox 10, 11, 15, 17, 31, 39, 49

Safety 13, 17, 21, 37, 40, 41
Speed 7, 11, 21, 22, 28, 42, 59
Speedometer 15, 17, 21, 37, 39, 41, 48, 49
Speedster 3, 9, 15, 17
Splash pans 31
Split pins (cotter pins) 13, 40
Springs 10, 26, 36, 39, 40
Starting 6, 11, 17, 21, 22, 29, 30, 33, 34, 41, 42
Steering 9, 22, 26, 39, 40-42, 53

Technical forums 51, 55
Timer (commutator) 8, 10, 13, 21, 32, 53
Tires (tyres) 7, 10, 22, 25, 26, 39, 53
Ton Truck (TT) 3, 6, 7, 15, 21, 25-28, 35, 59
Tools 26, 39, 40, 50
Touring Car 3, 4, 6-9, 14, 22, 36-38, 50, 58, 59
Town Car 6, 7, 14
Transmission (stock) 6, 30, 31, 42
Trim 22, 36, 38, 51
True Fire 21, 32
Tudor 14

Valuations 46
Values 8, 14, 16, 48
Van 15
Viewing 16, 21, 43
VIN 18, 45

Warford gearbox 10, 11, 15, 17, 31, 39, 49
Water pump 24, 28, 30
Wheels 12, 13, 20-22, 25, 26, 39, 49, 51, 54
Windshield (windcsreen) 37, 41
Windshield wiper 37
Wings (fenders) 10, 35-38

64